✦ JULIE DANNEBERG ✦

Women Writers
of the West

FIVE CHRONICLERS OF THE AMERICAN FRONTIER

FULCRUM PUBLISHING
GOLDEN, COLORADO

To my mother,
Margaret Egan Poremba

Notable Western Women Series
ISBN 1-55591-464-0
ISSN 1544-3779

Printed in the United States of America
0 9 8 7 6 5 4 3 2 1

Editorial: Marlene Blessing and Daniel Forrest-Bank
Design: Trina Stahl
Formatting: Patty Maher
Cover photograph: Portrait of Mary Hallock Foote, courtesy the Denver Public Library Western History Collection. Text excerpted from a letter written by Mary Hallock Foote.

Fulcrum Publishing
16100 Table Mountain Parkway, Suite 300
Golden, Colorado 80403
(800) 992-2908 • (303) 277-1623
www.fulcrum-books.com

Contents

Introduction

In this book, *Women Writers of the West*, you are going to meet five independent, adventurous, stubborn, and exasperating women. Five women driven to write and succeed at a time when ambition in women was viewed as a flaw, not an asset. Although most of their writing occurred more than a hundred years ago, many of their works—poems, stories, novels, and essays—have lasted and can still be read and enjoyed today.

Thanks to Jessie Benton Fremont's vivid descriptions (penned under her husband's name), we can still follow her husband's famous expeditions across the unexplored frontier West. Louise Clappe's exuberant letters home share the happiness and hardship of life in a remote California mining camp. Accomplished illustrator and writer Mary Hallock Foote helped her audience experience the West through her words and her pictures. Helen Hunt Jackson wrote lilting poems and descriptive essays filled with the beauty of the West. She also wrote hard-hitting, fact-filled reform literature about the ugliness of America's Indian policy, including an unforgettable novel on the subject, *Ramona*. Finally, Sioux writer Gertrude Bonnin's autobiographical stories reveal the sweetness of her childhood in South Dakota and the bitterness of leaving that life for a government school in Indiana.

The biographies in this book are not comprehensive life stories. Rather, they are meant to introduce you to each woman as she discovers the West on her own terms. And just as the West's culture molded these women's personalities and viewpoints, it also shaped their writing as they drew on the power of these new impressions and experiences as material for their different writings. Their works are filled with vivid descriptions of the West's magnificent scenery, sympathetic introductions to local characters and communities, and fascinating glimpses into the realities of home and hearth, but with a decidedly frontier flare.

While you are reading *Women Writers of the West*, it is important to realize that this book is a work of creative nonfiction. Although the facts, places, dates, and events are accurate, the means used to communicate them is fictional narrative. The words you read from each individual are not exact quotes, but instead are the author's creative rendering of what might have been said based on actual facts. A bibliography at the end of each chapter provides sources for further information on each woman.

The purpose of this book is to offer a deeper understanding of how each writer was shaped by the West, by showing her life in relationship to the time, geography, and culture in which her writing was produced. So, by switching between first and third person, the book offers the reader the unusual opportunity to see the West through the eyes and experiences of each of these writers, as well as observing each writer through the eyes of the West.

Women Writers
of the West

⁓

FIVE CHRONICLERS OF THE AMERICAN FRONTIER

Jessie Benton Fremont

(1824–1902)

G LAMOROUS, WEALTHY, and powerful. These three words best describe Jessie Benton Fremont. She and her husband, John Charles Fremont, were one of the most recognized and admired couples in the United States during the mid-nineteenth century.

Jessie Benton Fremont was born on May 31, 1824, one of six children to powerful Missouri Senator Thomas Benton and his southern wife Elizabeth McDowell. Growing up, Jessie felt especially close to her father. An involved yet unconventional father, Senator Benton often bucked the traditional beliefs of the time when raising his children. He insisted that his daughters, as well as his sons, receive an education. He saw to it that the girls did not wear the dainty slippers and confining clothing of the times, but instead bought them sturdy shoes and sensible dresses and then encouraged

John Fremont swept Jessie off her feet with his rugged good looks. Reproduced by permission from the Collections of the Library of Congress.

OPPOSITE: *Jessie Benton Fremont in 1856. Illustration courtesy of the Southwest Museum, Los Angeles (#N30665).*

Headstrong

In 1838, fifteen-year-old Jessie was already being sought as a bride by Washington, D.C., bachelors. As a way to avoid marriage for several more years, Senator Benton sent her to Miss English's Seminary for Girls, a fashionable boarding school located in Georgetown, three miles outside of Washington, D.C. Right from the start Jessie detested the confining, wealthy atmosphere. When Senator Benton asked about his daughter's progress the principal wrote, "Miss Jessie, although extremely intelligent, lacks the docility of a model student. Moreover, she has the objectionable manner of seeming to take our orders and assignments under considerations, to be accepted or disregarded by some standard of her own." In other words, Jessie was smart, lively, and unafraid to think for herself.

them to run and play. He valued and nurtured Jessie's independence and intelligence at a time when girls were not supposed to be independent or intelligent.

The daughter of a rich senator, Jessie grew up in a world of privilege and power. As a child she often accompanied her father to his office in the Capitol, had free reign of the congressional library, and was included in his visits to the White House to see his good friend, President Andrew Jackson.

When Congress was in session, the family lived in Washington, D.C., enjoying the hustle and bustle of the thriving city. During the rest of the year they alternated their time between Mrs. Benton's family plantation in the South and the senator's home in the frontier town of St. Louis.

Gradually Jessie grew from a high-spirited tomboy to a beautiful, headstrong young woman. When her best friend was married off to a man much older, Jessie cut her long hair in protest. When Jessie was told to behave properly at a family wedding, she promptly changed outfits with a male cousin and scandalized everyone by appearing in public dressed as a boy. Finally, against her parent's wishes, Jessie fell in love with John Charles Fremont, a penniless explorer with a wanderer's taste for adventure.

SENATOR BENTON: WASHINGTON, D.C., OCTOBER 1841

Damnation! That scoundrel John Charles Fremont eloped with my daughter!

When Mrs. Benton and I first noticed the sparks of romance between Jessie and John, we tried to separate them. Why, with her background and good looks, she could have married any man in Washington, D.C. But from the moment they met, those two only had eyes for each other.

When seeking to marry without Senator Benton's consent, Jessie and John found their choices somewhat limited. John unsuccessfully approached a Protestant minister as well as the mayor of Washington, D.C. Finally, although neither of them were Catholic, they found a priest who agreed to perform the ceremony. Later, in a letter to a close friend, Jessie described the ceremony this way: "Civil contract only, I should say. It was in a drawing room—no altar lights or any such thing—I was asked nothing but my age—and the whole thing was very short."

"Wait a year before you think of marriage," I ordered them. But instead, they met secretly for walks in the park and dinner with friends. Finally, they snuck off to marry! How dare they?

"Out of my house!" I thundered at John when the two of them finally confessed to their treachery. Of course, it was a mistake to think I could bully Jessie into doing something she didn't want to. With fire in her eyes, she stood firm and refused to let John go.

"Fine!" I yelled. "Then you both must leave!" And they did.

ELIZABETH BENTON: NOVEMBER 1841

What a scene! Never has the Senator been so angry, not that I blame him. Jessie's headstrong behavior hurt both of us. And can you believe it? She was angry at us, saying we were the ones acting unreasonably. For weeks the Senator raged, and for weeks I begged him to forgive Jessie's impetuous behavior. Thank goodness his anger eventually cooled. But then, I knew he couldn't stay mad at Jessie forever. Hadn't she always been the special light of his life? Finally, he invited the wayward couple back into our lives and into our home. They moved into a lovely room overlooking the garden.

GOSSIP

Former President Martin Van Buren once called Washington, "the gossipingest place in the world." Regarding the society women so concerned with everyone's business, President Andrew Jackson said, "I had rather have live vermin on my back than the tongue of one of these Washington women on my reputation."

GUEST AT PRESIDENT JOHN TYLER'S NEW YEAR'S DAY RECEPTION: JANUARY 1, 1842

Like many other Washington, D.C., citizens I looked forward to attending the president's annual New Year's Day party. An ordinary woman like myself didn't often get the chance to rub elbows with the rich and famous. The sparkling winter sunshine warmed us as, one by one, private carriages rattled up to the White House steps to deposit their guests. Of course, the grandest entrance of all was made when John Fremont himself stepped out, stunningly handsome in his glittering army uniform. A murmur rustled through the crowd as he turned back and extended his hand to Jessie, who stepped down from the carriage holding the skirt of her narrow-hooped, blue velvet gown. Atop her head three large ostrich feathers bobbed fashionably in her bonnet.

"What nerve they have, appearing out in public," I heard one old woman say disapprovingly.

"There is nothing disgraceful about being in love," I wanted to snap back, but I held my tongue as I watched John and Jessie disappear into the White House.

JESSIE

It was such fun stepping down from that carriage. I giggled when I heard gasps come up from the crowd. Did they expect John and I to hide away forever? What did I care if the Washington gossips didn't approve of our marriage? As if it mattered to me that John was born poor and illegitimate. I didn't care one whit about his background. I already saw the hero in him, and some day, I knew, the rest of the world would too.

A Female Politician

Growing up in a political home, Jessie spent her childhood observing the behavior of many politicians. She learned the importance of putting on a good show, concealing her true emotions, and making friends with her worst enemies. Jessie's knowledge of politicians and politics served her husband well throughout their marriage. On August 30, 1861, when John was serving as a major general commanding the Department of the West, he issued this nation's first Emancipation Proclamation. Even though Fremont only freed the slaves of the Missouri rebels, President Lincoln did not support his actions and ordered him to rescind the proclamation. John refused and sent Jessie to Washington to plead his case with the president. Lincoln, not particularly happy to have a woman acting in this capacity, said to Jessie, "You are quite a female politician." Jessie later wrote, "I felt the sneering tone and saw the foregone decision against all listening."

John Charles Fremont

I admit to feeling a bit daunted by the guest list that day, a regular "who's who" of Washington, D.C., politics and society. And there in the midst of past and current presidents, generals, and senators stood my Jessie, greeting, conversing, and laughing with some of the most powerful men in the country. She looked as comfortable and self-assured as if she was standing in her own parlor. I already loved her active mind and unbounded energy, but at that moment I knew that Jessie was the partner to help me make my dreams come true.

Jessie: Washington, D.C., New Year's Day, 1842

That night, after the president's reception, we returned to father's house for a family dinner. As the servants silently bustled around us, Father shared his good news. "I have finally

Go West, Young Man

In 1841, the area extending northwest from the Rocky Mountains to the Pacific Ocean was called Oregon Country and was owned jointly by Great Britain and the United States since an 1818 treaty. Senator Benton believed that whichever nation settled this region would eventually control it. He felt it was the government's job to promote and aid western expansion. In 1843, he told the senate, "Emigration is the only thing which can save the country from the British." Senator Benton hoped that John's expeditions would be the beginning of an effort to do just that.

persuaded Congress to fund an expedition to map out the land between the Mississippi River and the Rocky Mountains," he exclaimed, eyes alight with excitement. And then, looking right at John he said, "And I want you to help lead that expedition, Son." Such excitement! We all raised our glasses in good cheer, welcoming a year already rich with new opportunities.

JOHN: SPRING 1842

Of course, along with the joy of leading the expedition came the responsibility of planning and organizing it. My mind swirled, trying to keep track of all the details involved in putting together a four-month trip into the wilderness. I had to hire at least twenty-five men; gather animals for the trip; buy food and supplies, weapons and ammunition; and think about what scientific instruments I'd need to take with me. Luckily, I had Jessie to help. We began almost at once, plotting and planning, making lists, writing letters, and gathering supplies. As word of the expedition spread, Senator Benton's house was overrun with visitors. Inventors demonstrated their latest gadgets. Salesmen showed up at the doorstep hawking their wares. Young men volunteered their services, while old men volunteered their advice. Besides taking over much of my correspondence, I put Jessie in charge of handling all those visitors.

INVENTOR

I visited John Fremont, wanting to show him my invention in the hopes that he'd use it on his expedition. But before I even got in the door, his wife peppered me with questions. "What does a woman know about science?"

CALIFORNIA DREAMING

By the time John set out on his expedition, a few hopeful emigrants had already reached California. In November 1841, a group consisting of thirty-two men and an eighteen-year-old woman with her baby daughter arrived in the San Joaquin Valley after a long and dangerous journey. In her book Jessie Benton Fremont, *Pamela Herr related their adventures: "Traveling with only the vaguest directions, they had been forced to abandon their wagons in the sandy wastes beyond the Great Salt Lake and eat their pack animals for food as they struggled to find their way over the Sierra Nevada. 'Our ignorance of the route was complete,' one of them later confessed. 'We knew that California lay west and that was the extent of our knowledge.'" John's two expeditions gave later emigrants the information they needed to make the trip more safely.*

I answered rudely. Well, that little lady showed me to the door before I even got to speak to Lieutenant Fremont. I voiced my concerns to Senator Benton when he walked by. The old man just threw back his head and laughed. "That's my Jessie," he said as he walked away.

JESSIE: WASHINGTON, D.C., SPRING 1842

As the day for John's departure approached, I found that my moods changed by the minute. Mother said it was because I was pregnant. But I knew it was more than that. One minute I was bubbling over with joy, proud of John's success and hopeful for our future. The very next moment my feelings swung the other way. Yes, John was doing what he loved, but where did that leave me? I felt jealous knowing that he would soon be off on the adventure that we had planned together. I dreaded being tucked into the background,

No News Is No News

In this modern day of instant communication, it is hard to imagine how out of touch with their family and friends the men of the expedition were. After all, the group was traveling beyond the boundaries of civilization. Once in awhile, the group came across a trapper or trader in the middle of nowhere. If they were lucky, this wanderer might be going in the direction of their home and might agree to carry a letter. But this kind of mail handling was often unreliable. John wrote regularly to Jessie, and when the opportunity arose, sent a whole packet of letters home. Unfortunately, the man carrying the bundle of letters lost them when fording a stream.

As Jessie listened to John's stories of the frontier, she undoubtedly pictured his adventures in her mind. Illustration courtesy of the Denver Public Library Western History Collection.

alone, awaiting the birth of our child. Some days I regretted desperately not being a man.

SENATOR BENTON: WASHINGTON, D.C., SUMMER 1842

My strong, unflappable Jessie fell apart when John left. The fire went right out of her. And, of course, it didn't help matters when Mrs. Benton had a stroke and I turned to my Jessie to help run the house and care for her mother. Poor Jessie. She no longer made the round of parties, dances, and plays that she and John had attended so enthusiastically throughout the spring. She couldn't sleep and dark shadows appeared under her eyes. "I didn't think waiting would be this hard," she confided to me. I could see that she needed something to take her mind off her worries. Finally, one day, I led her into my study, sat her down at the library table, and said, "You are too young and too bright to fritter your days away." So each morning, Jessie worked for me, translating documents, writing letters, or doing research. It turned out we needed each other's help.

Jessie: Washington, D.C., Fall 1842

John returned safe and sound on October 29, 1842. Our daughter Lily was born on November 15. Once the ordeal of childbirth was over, John burst into my room, his face raw with emotion. With a flourish, he unfurled the wind-tattered flag of his expedition and laid it across my bed. "I placed this flag on one of the highest peaks in the Rocky Mountains and now I lay it at your feet."

John

The last responsibility of my expedition was to provide the government with a report of my scientific findings and experiences. The joy of accomplishment I felt at completing the journey soon gave way to utter frustration and despair. Day after day I sat at my desk waiting for the words to come, and day after day those words escaped me. Whenever I sat down to write, my head throbbed, my stomach rolled and bubbled, and my temper flashed. "I can't do it," I said, and in defeat, set the report aside.

Jessie

My heart ached as I watched John struggle with the task of writing his report. Too many nights by the campfire, too many hours on horseback, too much freedom had robbed him of the ability to sit quietly at a desk hour upon hour. "Why don't you tell me about your journey, and I'll write it down for you," I suggested. And so we began our collaboration, with John pacing the room and dictating words about his trip.

I noticed that after a few days our collaboration changed. I no longer just wrote down

A Special Flag

The flag that John gave Jessie was the special flag that she had designed and made for his expedition. It looked somewhat like the American flag with thirteen red and white stripes and twenty-six stars surrounding an eagle holding a peace pipe in its talons. The peak where John Fremont so proudly placed his flag is in the Wind River Range in present-day Wyoming. That peak is now known as Mount Fremont.

He Made It!

The moment John Fremont reached what is known as Mount Fremont in Wyoming was described in the report as follows: "Here, on the summit, where the stillness was absolute, unbroken by any sound and the solitude complete, we thought ourselves beyond the region of animated life; but while we were sitting on the rock, a solitary bee came winging his flight from the eastern valley and lit on the knee of one of the men."

As the bee flew away, John snapped his journal shut, capturing the bee forever in the pages of history.

his exact words. Instead, I often stopped John, prodding him with questions to elicit more information. I tried to picture in my mind the scenes he was describing, and I asked for more details. Soon, I understood that I needed to write more than just a list of dates and places and facts. Of course, the experiences and knowledge belonged to John, but the task of shaping those experiences into words that others could easily read with enjoyment was a task shared by both of us. I wanted to make sure that John's enthusiasm and his sense of adventure came through the writing. I wanted the reader to feel John's exhilaration as he hunted down his first buffalo, to shiver with him as he rode for hours in a cold drizzling rain, and to feel the camaraderie around the campfire on a star-studded night.

ELIZABETH BENTON

Every morning, Jessie left the baby with a nurse and disappeared into the Senator's study to work with John. It was just like Jessie to try and take over a man's work instead of just concentrating on being a mother. "Such strenuous mental exercise is not good for a woman," I warned Jessie over and over again, shaking my head with disapproval. I even asked the Senator to make her put aside such foolishness. But he refused to interfere. "Without Jessie's help, John won't finish the report, and we need that report," he explained.

JESSIE

To tell the truth I never felt better than during those long hours of writing. I woke up every morning eager to begin the day's work. I loved spending time with John, but I also relished the chance to participate in something that, according to Father, might shape the future of this country.

We began our work at nine in the morning. John brought his journal and maps from the expedition. As he spoke, he paced restlessly around the room, gesturing and grimacing as he relived each day's events in his mind. Through my writing, I took the trip with John. I wrote furiously, thinking hard, and by lunchtime we were both exhausted from our travels.

John and I made the perfect team. This project took his actions and my words and mixed them into one seamless match.

Colonel John J. Abert, Chief of the Topographical Corp.: March 1, 1843

Lieutenant Fremont turned in his report of the expedition. It was two hundred seven pages long, and I read it expecting the usual dry scientific report. Instead, to my surprise, I found myself caught up in a grand adventure story. The report was written in his wife's clear, easy-to-read handwriting. And although it had John's name signed to it, I believe the words also belonged to his wife, Jessie.

After reading and enjoying every word, I recommended to the Senate that we publish it as a senate document along with an extra thousand copies for the general public, in case anyone was interested.

Seventeen-Year-Old Boy: Cincinnati, Summer 1843

In case anyone was interested?! Well, I couldn't have been more interested! Historians say that Fremont's report fired up the imagination of the country. I know for sure that it fired up mine. A neighbor loaned me his copy, and after I read it, I could hardly think of anything else. I was supposed to be sweeping floors and stocking shelves in my father's store, but in my head I was chasing buffalo across the grassy plain and sitting with Indian chiefs before a flickering fire.

Jessie vs. John

How much of the report was created by John and how much was created by Jessie? This has remained a controversial question. Pamela Herr discusses this controversy in her well-researched book, Jessie Benton Fremont. *"While John's observation and experience formed its solid core, Jessie's hand can be seen in its graceful style, the skillful pacing, and the vivid scenes and vignettes that make it so readable. Without her sharp eye for a good story, the report, if completed at all, would have been a dry treatise to be filed and forgotten."*

A popular, sociable couple, John and Jessie enjoyed the sights of Washington, D.C. Reproduced by permission from the Collections of the Library of Congress.

Pa admitted I was useless around the shop, and finally, after much persuading, he let me head west too.

JESSIE

John received a lot of attention for that book. The senators all came around, slapping him on the back and congratulating him for his huge success. Excerpts from our report appeared in newspapers all over the country. It didn't bother me that my part wasn't acknowledged in the writing of the book, that my name wasn't on the cover. People don't read books written by women. Besides, it was John's story. A wife's place is to work behind the scenes, not to try and steal the show from her husband. But I learned something important in the writing of that book. I enjoyed the attention of being Mrs. John Charles Fremont. And I saw how my talents helped John with his career. If I couldn't be ambitious for myself, well then, what is wrong with putting all my energy behind the ambitions of my husband?

In their telling of the expedition, John and Jessie made both the mundane and the dangerous seem exciting: "July 3—Having travelled twenty-five miles, we encamped at 6 in the evening; and the men were sent across the river for wood, as there is none here but dry excrement of the buffalo, ... Wolves in great numbers surrounded us during the night, crossing and recrossing from the opposite banks to our camp, and howling and trotting about in the river until morning. July 4—While we were at breakfast, a buffalo calf broke through the camp, followed by a couple of wolves. In its fright it had probably mistaken us for a band of buffalo. The wolves were obliged to make a circuit around the camp, so that the calf got a little start, and strained every nerve to reach a large herd at the foot of the hills, about two miles distant: but first one, and then another, and another wolf joined in the chase, until his pursuers amounted to twenty or thirty, and they ran him down before he could reach his friends."

—The Exploring Expedition to the Rocky Mountains

❧ Afterword ❧

ALMOST AS SOON AS Jessie and John completed that first report, they began planning and organizing for the next expedition, which ended with their second successful collaboration in 1845.

John's third expedition to California didn't fare as well, however. After two years away, he returned home in 1847 amidst political scandal over his involvement in the United States war with Mexico. Even this humiliation did not quench the public's love for and fascination with both John and Jessie. John quit the army and found private funding for yet another expedition to California. This time, however, Jessie traveled by boat through the Isthmus of Panama, one of the first women 49ers, determined to meet John at the end of his journey. They planned to make a new start. In 1850, when politics called, John left for Washington as California's newly elected United States senator. Jessie and the children followed.

After failing to get re-elected for a second term, John Fremont and his family returned to their ranch in California. Although Jessie and John faced

In May 1843, John set out on another expedition with orders to survey and map a route from Wyoming to California. Upon his return, John and Jessie once again collaborated on the report. When this report went to press, it was combined with the first one into a single book. Ten thousand copies were printed and met with the same enthusiastic response from John's fans. John and Jessie's book, The Exploring Expedition to the Rocky Mountains, *although written more than 150 years ago, still makes good reading and is still available in bookstores and libraries.*

defeat in the political world, in their private lives they were becoming rich. Gold had been found on their California ranch, at one point earning them over $37,000 a month.

In 1856, John was asked to be the first presidential candidate for the newly formed Republican Party. Of course, Jessie stood beside him, becoming the first active and highly visible candidate's wife in a presidential campaign. People were attracted to her charisma. The campaign slogans praised "Fremont and Our Jessie."

Ultimately, John's moneymaking schemes soured. Nothing was left but for Jessie to pick up her pen once again, this time to pay the bills, and to feed and clothe her family. She wrote essays and stories that detailed the history she had witnessed firsthand. From privileged and pampered child to famous society matron, from adventurous traveler to hardworking career woman, Jessie had lived a life full of exceptional experiences, and the public wanted to read about them.

The rest of Jessie's life with John continued as it began, full of glorious victories and tragic defeats. But no matter what the circumstances, Jessie always rose to the occasion. Whether as a devoted mother of three, a successful writer, a dutiful wife, or a behind-the-scenes powerhouse, Jessie tackled everything with energy, courage, and grace. She once said, "I am like a deeply built ship. I drive best under a strong wind."

~ Bibliography ~

Egli, Ida Rae, ed. *No Rooms of Their Own: Women Writers of Early California; 1849–1869.* Berkeley, Calif.: Heyday Books, 1997.

Fremont, John C. *The Exploring Expedition to the Rocky Mountains.* Washington, D.C.: Smithsonian Institution Press, 1988.

Harris, Edward D. *John Charles Fremont and the Great Western Reconnaissance.* New York: Chelsea House, 1990.

Herr, Pamela. *Jessie Benton Fremont.* Norman, Okla.: University of Oklahoma Press, 1987.

Morrison, Dorothy Nafus. *Under a Strong Wind: The Adventures of Jessie Benton Fremont.* New York: Atheneum, 1983.

Phillips, Catherine Coffin. *Jessie Benton Fremont: A Woman Who Made History.* Lincoln, Nebr.: University of Nebraska Press, 1990.

Riley, Glenda, and Richard W. Etulain, eds. *By Grit & Grace: Eleven Women Who Shaped the American West.* Golden, Colo.: Fulcrum Publishing, 1997.

Seagraves, Anne. *High-Spirited Women of the West.* Hayden, Id.: Wesanne Publications, 1992.

Worth, Richard. *Westward Expansion and Manifest Destiny in American History.* Berkeley Heights, N.J.: Enslow Publishing, 2001.

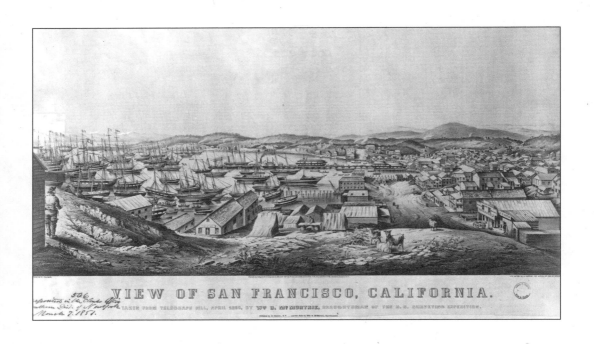

VIEW OF SAN FRANCISCO, CALIFORNIA.

TAKEN FROM TELEGRAPH HILL, APRIL 1851, BY W.ᵐ B. McMURTRIE, DRAUGHTSMAN OF THE U. S. SURVEYING EXPEDITION.

Published by H. Bainbridge, N.Y. and Sold, Only by Mrs. R. McMurtrie, San Francisco.

Louise Amelia Knapp Smith Clappe

(1819–1906)

T HINK FOR A MOMENT about a woman in the gold seeker's West. What kind of picture pops into your mind? For many, it's a grainy black-and-white image of a tight-lipped woman in a shapeless dress, standing in front of a rickety log cabin. Lines of fatigue crease her face. Her shoulders sag under the weight of the unpleasantness of her daily life.

Unfortunately, there are no surviving photographs of Louise Amelia Knapp Smith Clappe. If there were, though, you might see a different image than the stereotypical woman of the early West. True, this pretty blonde might have lived in a rickety log cabin, and she certainly faced hardships during her time in the California camps. But the fact is, Louise Clappe didn't resent mining camp life, she relished it.

Born to intellectually active, financially secure parents in Elizabethtown, New Jersey, Louise was the oldest of seven children. Her parents loved and nurtured her. Louise's father died when she was twelve, and six years later her mother died. Luckily, family members stepped

SOPHISTICATED CITY

B y 1851, San Francisco was a city with many comforts and conveniences. In her book, They Saw the Elephant: Women in the California Gold Rush, JoAnn Levy quotes Mary Crocker, a gold rusher's wife. Arriving in San Francisco, Mary was impressed by the sophisticated city. "I saw a larger variety of the richest things of all kinds than I ever did before. Beautiful embroideries, silks and satins, carving in ivory…. I saw splendid jewelry, too, one Pin for $2,000, one for $800, another for $6,000. Diamond bracelets, pins and rings, that is a grand place for a person to go who does not know how to dispose of his money."

OPPOSITE: *San Francisco was a booming city in 1850. Reproduced from the Collections of the Library of Congress.*

in to help raise the children, and eighteen-year-old Louise managed to finish her schooling. After graduation, she traveled around New England, taught school, and continued with her studies.

Louise's life changed when she met and married Fayette Clappe, an adventurous, often sickly young man who was finishing up his medical training. Within a year, the newlyweds were sailing around the horn of South America on their way to San Francisco, where Fayette hoped to work as a doctor. Instead, he spent much of their first year in California suffering from one illness after another. In the spring of 1851, Fayette decided to try his hand at mining camp medicine, so the couple traveled north through Sacramento to Marysville, California. Louise waited while Fayette continued into the mountains to explore work possibilities. During this waiting period, Louise began writing. On April 8, 1851, Louise's first essay was published in the *Herald*, the earliest newspaper north of Sacramento. Two essays and two poems followed in short order. Louise, in keeping with the tradition of the times, signed her articles with the "nom de plume," or pen name, of Dame Shirley.

By the summer of 1851, Fayette decided to spend the coming winter in a mining camp. Louise eagerly packed her belongings and accompanied him to the diggings.

San Francisco Friend: Late Summer 1851

"Spending the winter in the mountains? Are you crazy?" I asked Louise when she told me of her plans to move up to the mining camp of Rich Bar. "Don't you know that most miners come down to the flatlands for the snow months?" I reeled off a list of dangers, including snow-covered peaks that blocked the passes and rain-flooded rivers that clogged the valleys with mud. Add to that the possibility of starvation, loneliness, and plain boredom. And what about being one of the only young women in a camp full of rowdy miners? "Don't go!" I pleaded, but Louise just smiled and continued her packing.

LOUISE: SAN FRANCISCO, FALL 1851

It's true, my friends thought I was crazy for leaving the comforts and conveniences of San Francisco. Many thought I should just let my husband, Fayette, go to the diggings by himself. But I didn't travel all the way from New England just to live alone in San Francisco. Besides, why should Fayette be the only one to have adventures?

FAYETTE: MARYSVILLE, SEPTEMBER 8, 1851

We rested in Marysville for a few days before continuing on our journey. I worried about Louise riding the mule for such a great distance, and so, against her wishes, I arranged for the stagecoach to carry her to Bidwell's Bar, our next stop some thirty-nine miles away.

LOUISE

As Fayette rode out of town, leading my mule, I climbed into a box of a stagecoach. Oh the discomfort of it! Every rut, rock, and rough spot jarred my seat, and with no springs to absorb the shock, I was endlessly bounced and jostled. My body ached all over.

After many miles, we left the flatlands and made our way into the mountains. The winding road narrowed and the driver slowed down as the stagecoach wheels teetered along the edge, sending rocks skittering over the cliff. Upon looking out and seeing nothing but jagged boulders far below, I scooted to the far side of the stagecoach bench and held my breath.

STAGECOACH DRIVER

That Mrs. Clappe was a tiny thing. I sure 'nuff expected her to start screaming the minute the road narrowed. Most women do, ya know. Truth be told, they aren't fit for this kind of travelin'. But Mrs. Clappe never let out a peep. I do believe she was the first woman I've taken over that pass who didn't cry and carry on.

SPINSTER WOES

On September 10, 1848, thirty-year-old Louise Clappe was saved by the bell—the wedding bell that is. Unmarried older women in Louise's time looked forward to a life of dependence and insecurity. Victorian society frowned on women who worked for a living, believing that to do so was vulgar and improper behavior. However, without an income, single women depended on others to feed, clothe, and house them. They lived with aging parents or with married brothers or sisters. Unmarried women often had no permanent home, but instead occupied the guest room in other people's homes, moving from one relative to another as their welcomes wore out.

FAYETTE

Louise's stagecoach arrived at three o'clock in the afternoon. Bidwell's Bar was bursting at the seams with expectant miners. We soon found that the only available accommodation was a dirty canvas tent. Upon closer inspection, Louise noticed that the black dirt covering the tent wasn't dirt at all but a mass of hopping, jumping, soon-to-be-biting fleas! "No thank you," we both said, and decided to continue on to Berry Creek House, a ranch some ten miles closer to our destination.

LOUISE

We rode out of town by moonlight. The air was soft and cool without a hint of dampness. Shadowed woods hemmed in the road. Filled with the thrill of our adventure, we laughed, sang songs, and told stories. But as the night lengthened, the trail closed in on us. The branches and bushes scratched and scraped so that we rode with our heads down against the neck of the mule. Nine o'clock came and went. I wondered why we didn't arrive. Ten o'clock, eleven, twelve. "Surely we should be there by now?" I asked Fayette. He assured me that the ranch was around the next bend. But it wasn't. As hour after hour passed, the darkness got deeper, the woods thicker, the trail thinner.

"We must be lost," Fayette finally admitted. I refused to continue one second more. Under the thin, smelly saddle blankets off our mules and a worn-out quilt, we huddled together in a makeshift bed and waited for the dawn.

RANCH OWNER

Those two greenhorns straggled up to the ranch in the early evenin'. Near as I could tell, they had been in the saddle going on twenty-four hours, not counting the little bit of shut-eye they caught in the woods. When they complained about bein' lost, I told 'em they were just lucky to tell the tale. A few weeks ago, a Frenchman and his wife were killed by Indians near the exact same place they camped.

LOUISE

Several more days of travel brought us to the end of the trail. Far below, twinkling in the setting sun, lay the quaint-looking town of Rich Bar. Of course, I found out soon enough that the distance hid the dust and garbage that clogged the street, the loud sounds of the barroom, and the offensive odors of unwashed men. But at that moment, before reality hit me square in the senses, my heart swelled with pride at the accomplishment of completing a journey that so many called impossible for a woman.

MINER: RICH BAR

At five o'clock in the evening, Mrs. Clappe rode into town with her husband. Ah, the joy of it! I hadn't seen one of the female persuasion for many a day. I shook my head at their arrival though. They were comin' into town when many of us experienced miners were headin' out. Things get mighty unpleasant in a mining town when there ain't no mining to be done. I wondered if she and that doctor husband of hers were brave or just plain stupid.

NATIVE AMERICANS

The California Gold Rush was anything but positive for Native Americans already living in the area. In 1852, approximately 100,000 Native Americans were living in California. A little more than twenty years later in 1873, nearly all the California tribes had been either wiped out or moved onto reservations. An 1851 statement from California's first governor, Peter Burnett, certainly didn't help matters. He said, "This is a war of extermination that will continue until the Indian race shall become extinct. It is beyond the power or wisdom of man to avert the inevitable destiny."

MOLLY (LOUISE'S SISTER): NEW ENGLAND, SEPTEMBER 13, 1851

"Is this truly my sister?" I asked myself when I read through Louise's letters. I could barely picture her in the middle of these strange and glorious adventures. She showed a strength and determination I don't think she even realized she had. I found myself reading her letters as I would read a novel, so interesting and yet so distant from my everyday New England life.

LOUISE: RICH BAR, SEPTEMBER 15

Riding down Rich Bar's main street, I counted about forty buildings, a ramshackle collection of houses, and businesses. There were, of course, log cabins, shacks made out of planks, and many canvas tents. I even saw a hut made out of pine boughs and covered with old calico shirts.

We quickly settled in at the Empire Hotel, a rather grand name for a not-so-grand establishment, although it was the town's only two-storied building, and it did have real glass windows. To my delight, I was greeted by the owners, Mr. and Mrs. Bancroft. Mrs. Bancroft had several children at home and was toting around a baby, born right there on the premises only two weeks before. Like many of the women I've met, the hard frontier life showed in the deep lines of her face, the fatigue in her eyes, and the roughness of her hands.

MRS. BANCROFT

I welcomed Mrs. Clappe with real pleasure and looked forward to conversations between chores. What a joy to talk to someone who cares about something other than gold. I quickly peppered her with questions, wanting to know about life outside this isolated little town. Prior to Louise's arrival, the valley's female population, including myself, topped out at four.

Just as Louise noticed in Rich Bar, mining towns were always a conglomeration of mix-and-match housing. Photograph courtesy of the Denver Public Library Western History Collection.

LOUISE: RICH BAR, SEPTEMBER 20

Soon after arriving, I visited Fayette at his medical office. "It's the most respectable business in town," he boasted. However, when I walked in, my eyebrows hit the ceiling, my chin hit the floor, and I laughed until I couldn't take a breath. This oh-so-respectable office, the nicest one in Rich Bar, was nothing but a barn of a building, without a wooden floor or a real glass window. The entire medical library consisted of five or six books, and although the stock of supplies seemed more than adequate, the bottles and vials were lined up on a shelf that looked like nothing more than a few sticks nailed to the wall.

Fayette: Late September 1851

Louise and I hadn't been in town long when I faced a critical test. I was requested to come to the aid of a local miner who had his leg crushed by a falling boulder six months earlier. Although an amputation was recommended at that time, the miner refused, retiring to his dirty shack, foolishly hoping that time and rest would heal his crushed limb. Unfortunately, as the months passed, his leg became very infected. The miner's problem? Without an operation he would surely die. My problem? As a new doctor in the area, my future success rested on not killing my first patient.

Louise

Fayette agreed to do the operation and promptly moved the miner from his unkempt hovel to a nice clean room at the Empire Hotel. Luckily, both of them survived the amputation, and I set about helping to nurse the poor young man back to health. At a precious price, we obtained milk from a nearby ranch and, for the next few days, the only nourishment our patient took was an occasional teaspoon of milk dribbled through his parched lips. I wiped his fevered brow with a cold, damp cloth and waved a fragrant pine bough above his head to create a slight breeze. Gradually, he regained his strength, but at a price. He eventually left Rich Bar much poorer than when he arrived.

WASHERWOMAN: RICH BAR, LATE SEPTEMBER 1851

Mrs. Clappe, the new doctor's wife, showed up at my doorstep one day with a parcel of laundry for me to wash. I took it gladly, and not just for the money. How delightful to be washing something other than gray long johns and red flannel shirts. She insisted on paying me the same prices for washing as she paid in San Francisco. Can you imagine paying eight dollars to have a dozen linen handkerchiefs washed and ironed?

PAY UP

Of course, doctors didn't work for free. Their skills came at a price and, just like today, patients often complained that they charged too much for their services. One miner said, "they will hardly look at a man's tongue for less than an ounce of gold." According to the book California Gold Rush: A Guide to California in the 1850s, *doctors in San Francisco charged 30 grams of gold for the initial checkup.*

RUB-A-DUB-DUB

In 1849, the very first washerwomen in San Francisco were Mexican and Indian women. Gathering to do laundry at a pond that became known as Washerwoman's Bay, these women lined up at the edge of the water to scrub clothes on their metal washboards. They kept fires going on the beach to boil the clothing and to heat the irons. Eventually, because the money was so good, a few men also joined their ranks. In her book, They Saw the Elephant: Women in the California Gold Rush, *JoAnn Levy quotes an early San Franciscan: "It was an amusing sight to see a great, burly, long-bearded fellow, kneeling on the ground with sleeves rolled up to the elbows and rubbing a shirt on the board with such violence that the suds flew." Although women continued to dominate the laundry profession in the mining camps, in San Francisco by 1853, Chinese men had taken over the trade.*

A Woman's Work

*I*n her book, Life During the Gold Rush, *Victoria Sherrow introduces the reader to hardworking Mary Ballou. In a letter to her son, Mary described some of the work that made up her day. Besides making soap, sewing, and raising her children, she also had many other jobs to do. "I am washing and ironing, sometimes I am making mince pie and apple pie and squash pies … making biscuits … making gruel for the sick … feeding my chickens."*

No Longer Timid

*B*efore her trip west, Louise *considered herself sickly. After arriving in California, in one of her letters to her sister she wrote, "And only think of such a shrinking, timid frail thing as I used to be. I like this wild and barbarous life. Here, at least, I have been contented."*

Louise

Rich Bar's washerwoman, or rather her husband, was the envy of all the miners. What made this woman such a treasure? Was it her beauty? No. Her intelligence? No. The fact that she was such a good mother? No. Although she may have had all of these qualities and more, what made this woman so desirable was that she earned her own way. As one miner put it, "Marrying might be a sight more economical if all women were like her." Indeed. Over the course of nine weeks, through her own labor, she earned nine hundred extra dollars by washing other people's clothing. Of course, this business was conducted in addition to all of her daily duties of cooking, baking, and cleaning. Ouch, my back ached as I pictured her as she hunched over a steaming tub of water and lugged around heavy piles of wet clothing.

Fayette: Early October 1851

Louise and I agreed that it was time to move out of the hotel. The smell of stale whiskey greeted us every morning, and the barroom noises serenaded us to sleep every night. The sounds of barking dogs, cussing miners, bragging gamblers and thumping mining equipment punctuated every hour of the day.

A Simple Life

*I*n one of her letters home, Louise wrote "Really, everybody ought to go to the mines, just *to see how little it takes to make people comfortable in the world."*

I paid to have a log cabin built in Indian Bar, a tiny community a half-mile up the river. We packed our clothing, trunks, and a few pieces of furniture in a borrowed wagon and headed out of town.

LOUISE

To get to Indian Bar, we journeyed along the river where miners called out their hellos, glad for an excuse to straighten their backs and stop their work. Some bent over rusted, flat-bottomed pans, while others shoveled dirt into wooden rockers. I returned their calls with cheerful waves but didn't dare take my eyes off the path. One misstep and I'd surely tumble into one of the abandoned mine shafts that littered the valley floor.

The dream of every miner was to have a gold pan like this—full of more than $3,000 worth of gold nuggets. Photograph courtesy of the Denver Public Library Western History Collection.

FAYETTE

I made our new long cabin as presentable as I could. To hide the shingles, I draped long pieces of white cloth to form a ceiling and to hide the rough logs, I hung large quantities of rose chintz over the walls. I also strung a curtain across the middle of the room to divide the bedroom from the rest of the house. The door was a piece of canvas and the window a two-by-two-foot glassless opening cut into the log.

LOUISE: INDIAN BAR, EARLY OCTOBER 1851

I loved my new home. Arranging furniture and bringing out my few knickknacks reminded me of playing house as a girl. For

GLASS WINDOWS

One of the nicest houses in the area belonged to several bachelor miners who came up with a cheap and unusual way to provide their home with much-desired glass windows. They cut a three-foot section of log and lifted it out. They then filled the open space with empty glass jars. The jars, when new, had been filled with brandied fruit.

Making Do to the Max

Survival in a mining camp often depended on two things: the ability to make the best of every situation, and the knowledge that neighbors helping neighbors was a necessary part of daily life. Louise reveals both traits in a funny story she shared with her sister: "Last night, one of our neighbors had a dinner party. He came in to borrow a teaspoon. 'Had you not better take them all?' I said. 'Oh no,' was the answer, 'that would be too much luxury. My guests are not used to it, and they would think I was getting aristocratic and putting on airs. One is enough: they can pass it round from one to the other.'"

a sofa, we covered a wooden bench with a length of cheerful plaid material. Four chairs from the Empire Hotel were tucked in under our pine table. The cribbage and chessboard were set up on a small table in the corner, and a beautiful rug covered at least some of the uneven floor. For warmth, we had a big stone fireplace and although it heated the room efficiently, its untidy construction looked like someone left a pile of rocks and mud in our living room. The mantle was a wooden beam covered with strips cut from tin cans, the dark lettering still on them. Our few books were arranged artfully in a candle box.

I so enjoyed the quiet in Indian Bar, spending part of each day working on the letters that I sent to my sister. Mind you, they weren't just careless scribbles or the jotting down of quick thoughts. I carefully planned and researched each letter, trying to

Sisterly Letters

Louise wrote her sister a total of twenty-three letters between September 13, 1851, and November 21, 1852. Some historians believe that Louise wrote these letters purely as a way to keep in touch with her sister. Others, however, think that Louise set out to write those letters with the express purpose of eventually getting them published. After all, she had already published several essays written in the same letter format. She made copies of each letter before she sent it to her sister. Finally, the research and time that Louise's letter-writing process took seems to indicate something more than casual communication. Interestingly enough, in 1873, the English travel writer Isabella Bird embarked on a three-month horseback trip through Colorado with the intention of publishing a book on her experiences. She, too, kept track of the sights and sounds of her trip through letters she sent home to her sister.

include details that clearly showed my rustic life. After I finished, I made a copy for myself. You see, I had plans for publishing once I returned to "civilization," as Molly called it.

NED: OCTOBER 20, 1851

It was my misfortune to work as a cook at the only hotel in Indian Bar. I spent my days slaving over a hot stove and rustling up tin plates of grub for hungry miners. Did they care about my culinary talent? No! I swear they'd eat their shoes if I poured a little gravy on them. I knew the Clappes would appreciate my skills.

LOUISE

Ned welcomed us with a meal. Everything was "done up right." He didn't overlook a single detail. He even spent his own money to buy material to make white napkins.

CAMP CUISINE

Mining camp cuisine was very limited. For the most part, miners ate preserved food such as dried fruit, pickles, dried beans, dried beef, and salt pork. They also depended on staples that did not spoil such as flour, sugar, and cornmeal. If a miner wanted fresh meat, he had to hunt for it and then be willing to eat whatever he caught, including raccoon, rabbit, or antelope. Many miners suffered from scurvy (a disease caused by vitamin C deficiency) as a result of their poor diets.

Of course, anyone who lived in a mining camp soon became an expert on "making do." But for a cook, making do was very difficult. There were no vegetables available except onions and potatoes, no fresh eggs or milk, and the meat was what a hunter could bring in. But somehow, despite all of those limitations, the meal Ned cooked for us was perfection.

FIRST COURSE: Oyster Soup
SECOND COURSE: Fried Salmon, caught from the river
THIRD COURSE: Roast Beef and Boiled Ham
FOURTH COURSE: Fried Oysters
VEGETABLES: Potatoes and Onions
PASTRY: Mince Pie and Pudding, made without eggs or milk
DESSERT: Madeira Nuts and Raisins
WINES: Claret and Champagne
Coffee

NED

Once I cooked the meal, I changed into a clean flannel shirt and served it. I worked too hard for some clumsy miner to botch things up.

Louise probably looked much like these Colorado boomtown women when she tried her hand at gold panning. Photograph courtesy of the Denver Public Library Western History Collection.

LOUISE

Seeing miners bent over their claims every day finally roused my curiosity. I decided to give gold panning a try. What hard and tedious work! One of the miners scooped up some dirt from the river bottom in his dented old pan and handed it to me with water sloshing over the sides. I swished and swirled it around and around, trying to get the water out, but keep the dirt in. At the conclusion of my experiment I had earned $3.25 in gold but had soaked a brand new pair of gloves, ripped my dress, and froze my hands to the bone.

≈ *Afterword* ≈

LOUISE CONTINUED TO LIVE in Indian Bar for another year, during which time she often witnessed and wrote about the darker side of mining camp life. As the winter rains came, the men could no longer work their mines and became bored, spending their time drinking and gambling. Violence broke out, and Louise witnessed hangings and mob attacks against minority miners. Despite experiencing the ugly side of mining camp life, she also enjoyed her new friendships, the beauty of the surrounding mountains, and her time spent researching and writing letters.

By November 1852, the riches had been mined out of the Feather River and most of the miners had moved on. The Clappes returned to San Francisco where their marriage floundered. Fayette left for Hawaii and then New England. Louise remained in San Francisco. Louise and Fayette Clappe divorced in 1856.

In 1854, a friend of Louise's published a magazine that featured articles from western writers. Louise's first letter appeared in the first edition of the magazine under the name of Dame Shirley. For the next 23 months, each edition carried one of Dame Shirley's letters. Western and eastern readers alike enjoyed their humor and realistic portrayal of California mining camp life.

Louise spent the rest of her years involved with literary activities, but she never again produced such fine writing as she did with her letters from the mining camps.

≈ *Bibliography* ≈

Blashfield, Jean F. *The California Gold Rush*. Minneapolis, Minn.: Compass Point Books, 2001.

Clappe, Louise Amelia Knapp Smith. *The Shirley Letters: From the California Mines, 1851–1852*. Berkeley, Calif.: Heyday Books, 1998.

Egli, Ida Rae, ed. *No Rooms of Their Own: Woman Writers of Early California: 1849–1869*. Berkeley, Calif.: Heyday Books, 1997.

Ferris, Julie. *California Gold Rush: A Guide to California in the 1850s*. New York: Kingfisher, 1999.

Ketchum, Liza. *The Gold Rush*. Boston: Little, Brown, 1996.

Levy, JoAnn. *They Saw the Elephant: Women in the California Gold Rush*. Hamden, Conn.: Archon Books, 1990.

Rawls, Jim. *Dame Shirley and the Gold Rush*. New York: Steck-Vaughn, 1993.

Sherrow, Victoria. *Life During the Gold Rush*. San Diego, Calif.: Lucent Books, 1998.

Stein, R. Conrad. *The California Gold Rush*. Chicago: Children's Press, 1995.

Mary Hallock Foote

(1847–1938)

❧❧

MARY HALLOCK FOOTE, known as "Molly" to family and friends, was a woman of contrasts. A native New Englander, through her stories and novels she became a leading voice of the West. Molly was a traditional Victorian woman, who ambitiously pursued and attained a successful career in the arts. And, as a devoted mother and wife, she often felt torn between her own artistic desires and the needs and demands of her husband and children.

Born on November 19, 1847, Molly grew up on a farm overlooking the Hudson River near Milton, New York. As a child Molly was recognized as the "artist" of the family, and her talent was nurtured and encouraged. Just short of her seventeenth birthday, in 1864 she left home to attend the School of Design for Women at Cooper Union in New York City. Living with her sister-in-law's family, Molly enjoyed the adventures of big city life. Despite the distractions, however, she worked hard and eventually decided to focus her efforts on woodcut illustration. By the time Molly was twenty years old, her illustrations began to appear in popular magazines. Glowing reviews brought in prestigious commissions.

Molly's life overflowed with family, friends, and meaningful work that fed her spirit and filled her purse. Then twenty-six-year-old Molly met Arthur Foote, the handsome young man who dreamed not of art and literature, but of traveling West.

ARTHUR: NEW YORK CITY, JANUARY 1, 1873

I was attending a house party in New York City. Tired of making small talk and needing a quiet moment to myself, I escaped into the parlor for a moment's peace. There, practically hidden in the corner of the couch, sat a beautiful young woman

OPPOSITE: *Molly might have looked prim and proper on the outside, but inside she was strong and determined. Photograph courtesy of the Denver Public Library Western History Collection.*

bent over a sketchbook. Her sparkling eyes and tousled pompadour enchanted me. I asked her name and permission to stay.

"My name is Molly," she answered, "But you can't talk to me. I have to work on these illustrations." I tried to be quiet, really I did, but I couldn't resist some get-acquainted conversation. When I asked about her sketches, Molly spoke enthusiastically of her art. "You're lucky to have found something you love," I said and told her about my dream of moving west to become a mining engineer.

MOLLY: MILTON, NEW YORK, 1874–1876

We met several times over the next year, with Arthur visiting my home and meeting my family in September. Despite our congeniality, the West still pulled at his heart. Before he left, he asked to exchange letters during his absence. I reluctantly agreed, but to tell the truth, I didn't see much point. My life, my family, my work, and my future were in the East. Our letters started, at first awkward and shy, but as the months passed, they became a way for us to get to know each other. We shared our hopes, our dreams, and each time, a little bit more of ourselves. Oh, you can be sure I let him know that I was not the waiting-around-kind. I told him about every one of my successes, whether it was a good review, a big paycheck, or a new commission. Arthur never minded my bragging, though. He told me he was proud of me. And as we started thinking that there might be a future for us, he promised never to interfere with my career.

ARTHUR: NEW ALMADEN, CALIFORNIA, FEBRUARY 1876

For two years, I spent my days moving from one raw mining camp to another. I took any job that earned a few dollars, getting paid mostly in experience. Some called my learning the school of hard knocks. I just called it part of my plan. With a lot of patience and hard work, I eventually landed a real job, one that I could be proud of. I became the resident engineer for the Quicksilver mine in New Almaden, California. Finally, I had a job with decent pay. Finally, I had a future. I wrote Molly a letter asking her to marry me. She agreed, but when I asked her to marry me in San Francisco she simply refused. "We will marry at home with my family," she insisted. I waited until February and eagerly returned East to meet my bride.

MOLLY: MILTON, NEW YORK, JULY 1876

After a two-week honeymoon, Arthur returned—alone—to California. I stayed behind for four months to finish an illustration commission and then I prepared to join him. "Have I made a terrible mistake?" I wondered as I packed, thinking about beginning a new life out west. My stomach fluttered with dread as I pictured saying good-bye, perhaps forever, to my dear family.

AN ENGINEER'S EXPERIENCE

During Arthur Foote's day, there were two ways to become an engineer: go to college and take courses or go west and learn through the school of hard knocks. Arthur chose the latter. He often said that "an engineer's capital is his experience," and he based many of his career decisions on his desire to gain not money, but more experience. One interesting job he had early in 1875 was helping survey San Francisco's Golden Gate Park.

QUITE AN ARTIST

Molly was a woodcut illustrator. After composing her picture on a piece of paper, she drew it again directly onto a block of wood with a specially prepared surface. When her drawing was done, it appeared as a black line drawing against a white surface. An engraver would then carve away all the white, leaving just the black lines that Molly had drawn. The end result looked something like a raised rubber stamp, which, when inked, would print her drawing onto paper.

HELENA DE KAY GILDER

Helena de Kay Gilder and Molly Hallock Foote could not have been more different, and yet they became lifelong friends in art school. Describing Helena in her book, A Victorian Gentlewoman in the Far West, Molly said "...her people belonged to the old aristocracy of New York. My people belonged to nothing but the Society of Friends.... She had spent her childhood abroad and spoke three languages. I 'one imperfectly.' She had lived in one of the famous capitals of Europe and walked its galleries among the Old Masters, while I was walking the 'old green hills' of the Hudson..."

Helena eventually married Richard Gilder, editor of Scribner's Monthly, a popular magazine of the time. They shared a similar background, and an interest in art and culture.

GOOD ADVICE

When Mary first traveled West to be an engineer's wife, both she and Arthur believed it to be a temporary situation. In a letter to Helena she wrote, "For us, a home here (in the West) for a few years is inevitable, so there is nothing for it but to make the best of it. The best is not at all bad; it is only that there are people in the East I love, who draw my thoughts and longing away from what I should be wrapped up in, here. The only way to come West happily is to embrace the country, people, life, everything."

Many a night my anxiety woke me with clammy skin and thumping heart. I confided my fears to my friend, Helena, saying, "No girl ever wanted to 'go west' less with any man, or paid a man a greater compliment by doing so."

HELENA: NEW YORK, JULY 1876

Molly and I had been best friends since art school. For us, art was not "just a hobby" to occupy us until we got married but a passion to carry us through life. That's why I worried when she told me of her plans to move West with Arthur. Please don't misunderstand my concerns. I liked Arthur, but I also knew how much Molly would be giving up to follow him West. It was hard enough for a woman to pursue an art career in the East. But in the West, with no publishing contacts or other artists nearby, I worried she might set her work aside. "Who will you talk to? Who will encourage you? What will inspire you?" I wanted to ask Molly, but I kept my concerns to myself as I hugged her good-bye and wished her luck.

LIZZIE

Mrs. Foote hired me to accompany her to California. I was employed to do the cooking and cleaning and modeling. That's right, modeling. Mrs. Foote used real people to pose for her pictures, and she was afraid that in the far-off West there would be no suitable models. I gladly signed up for the job being delighted to leave the East behind. I planned to take my little boy and make a new life for myself.

Mrs. Foote and I started out strangers, but you can't travel three thousand miles and spend seven days confined in a cramped railroad car compartment without getting to know a person right quick. I knew by the end of that first week that I was going to enjoy my new life. As for Mrs. Foote, I think she had second thoughts when we started out. Her family brought her to the station and she took her leave amidst a shower of hugs and kisses and well-wishes.

THE SCARLET LETTER

Before leaving Milton, Molly agreed to illustrate a gift edition of Nathaniel Hawthorne's book, The Scarlet Letter. *This classic novel about a young woman with a small child made Lizzie a perfect choice of model for Molly because, just like the main character in the book, Lizzie had a baby whom Molly used as a model as well. Molly finished the last of the drawings in spring 1877, just before the birth of her first child.*

NEW ALMADEN

The New Almaden Mine was located in the Santa Clara Valley, about 50 miles southeast of San Francisco. The town surrounding the mine had a population of about 1,000. All of the inhabitants obeyed, through their interactions and behavior, the rigid social structure created by differences in education, class, and ethnicity. In other words, the management lived in one camp, the English-speaking laborers in another, the Mexican miners in another village, and the Chinese in still another village. It was expected that Arthur and Molly would live with the mine management in the well-groomed little town at the bottom of the mountain. Although everyone was kind and friendly to Molly and Arthur, their friendships were limited by the fact that they didn't live with the rest of the miners or the mine owners.

MOLLY

Leaving New York was almost a relief. Once the pain of parting was behind me, I turned my eyes toward the West, toward Arthur and my future. The train rumbled through Chicago, and Omaha, past the Great Salt Lake, and over the Sierra Nevadas into San Francisco. Not content to watch the scenery whiz by the window, I roamed the railroad cars until I found the perfect spot on the top step of the rear platform. The rhythmic clatter of the wheels serenaded me and a cool wind blew back my hair. Sometimes, as the train chugged past farms or homesteads, I'd see a woman looking back longingly at me from her garden or field. The farther west we traveled, the more dramatic the scenery became, so different from my green river valley back home. The wide spaces of prairie rolled out to the horizon. Farther west, the mountains stretched up to tickle the belly of the sky. The hot air dried my skin and smelled like dust. On our last day, I got up at four o'clock in the morning to watch the scenery as we crossed

During her train trip west, Molly enjoyed looking at scenery such as this rugged view of Weber Canyon in Utah. Photograph courtesy of the Denver Public Library Western History Collection.

over the Sierra Nevadas. The golden morning light reflected off the peaks, and I faced the beauty of the West with a song of celebration in my heart.

ARTHUR: SUMMER 1876

I enjoyed showing Molly around San Francisco. We spent a few days in a fancy hotel, resting up and seeing the sights. "I like it here. The West isn't wild at all," Molly said, delighted with the fine food and international shopping. It's true, San Francisco was a lively, sophisticated city in 1876. But the real test came when we took the train to San Jose and then hired a private carriage to carry us to our new home in a little mining town called New Almaden.

LIZZIE

On the carriage ride to New Almaden, Mrs. Foote ooohed and aaahed over the passing scenery. As for me, I was more concerned with the scenery inside the carriage as I studied Mr. Foote, my new employer. Handsome, tall, and physically fit, he had a well-trimmed mustache and thick blond hair. He looked young, although his face had the weathered appearance of someone who had spent a lot of time outside. His kind eyes flashed with delight as he watched Mrs. Foote flit around like a schoolgirl.

QUICKSILVER

"Quicksilver" is another name for the reusable liquid metal known as mercury. The New Almaden Mine, named after the world's largest mercury mine in Spain, was the only source of mercury in California. Mercury, known for its ability to attract gold, draws even the smallest gold particles to itself in a magnetic-like action called amalgamation. This quality made it an invaluable tool for miners using sluice boxes. By placing the quicksilver at the base of the sluice box, or at the seams, those small particles of gold called "float" or "flour" gold would be captured by the mercury before they were washed out with the tailings.

MOTHER HALL: NEW ALMADEN, CALIFORNIA, JULY 1876

I ran a boardinghouse in the village, cooking and cleaning for the single men, including Arthur, until he up and got married. On a day so hot that the sun baked the earth to dry red dust, he returned with his new bride, Molly, a fancy artist from back East. Although she seemed nice enough, and I grew to like her very much, I chuckled under my breath when I met their servant, Miss Lizzie. "Why in the world do they need a maid?" I wondered to myself, thinking of their tiny cabin up the mountain. Arthur, reading the look on my face, explained that Miss Lizzie's main job was to model for Molly. That's nice, I thought, but I supposed the Missus will be putting her art aside soon enough. Time to start acting like a proper wife.

Company Town

New Almaden was a company town, which means that the mine owners not only hired the miners and paid their salaries, but also rented them their houses and owned the stores where they bought their food and supplies. This system, while being very lucrative for the mine owners, did not work out as well for the miners. Without competition, there was no motivation for the company store to charge fair prices. In her autobiography, A Victorian Gentlewoman in the Far West, Molly told the story of an old miner who had worked for the company for many years. His employment ended, however, when he bought a stove pipe from San Jose instead of buying it at the company store. In retaliation, the manager had the miner's home destroyed and his few possessions taken. As the final blow, notice was given that whoever assisted the miner would be treated as a sympathizer and would meet the same fate.

Molly

I clapped with delight when I saw our new home, tucked into the side of the mountain. A large porch hugged three sides of the house, and a hammock swung invitingly across one corner. Inside, dark paneled rooms proved a cool refuge from the glaring heat. Arthur showed Lizzie to her tiny room off the kitchen, while I peeked into cupboards and rearranged a vase of wildflowers on the table. The house was rough and rustic, but smelled of cleaning supplies and fresh paint.

A Later Meeting with Molly

In his memoir, Idaho of Yesteryear, Tom Donaldson described his first meeting with Molly. Although the visit took place in their Leadville cabin, the description gives us a good image of Molly's personality: "As we approached, we discerned a rustic porch made comfortable by armchairs built of barrels sawed in half, stuffed with straw and covered with gunny sacks. To the right a hammock swung lazily suggesting that an eastern woman, and a cultivated one, lived at the house.... Mrs. Foote put us at ease with her sweet manners.... She was dressed in white and rounded out a pleasing picture in contrast to rugged nature all about her home.... Mrs. Foote settled herself for a chat until her husband returned and my, my, how she did talk! She was well-read on everything and ripped out an intellectual go-as-you-please backed up by good looks and brightness."

I twirled around with my arms spread out, happy in the knowledge that Arthur and I were finally starting our new life together.

Lizzie
We settled down quickly into our new routine. I busied myself with running the house for the Footes while Molly filled her days with Arthur and her work. Early in the morning as the fog rolled back down the valley, she walked Arthur to his office in the village and then continued on to hike around the mountain.

Mary used her surroundings to inspire both her writing and illustrations. This is an etching of the Leadville, Colorado, cabin where she and Arthur lived so happily in the summer of 1879. Reproduced by permission of The Huntington Library, San Marino, California.

The rest of the day she spent drawing at the kitchen table.

MOLLY: NEW ALMADEN, FALL 1876

It's funny how things work out. That first year in New Almaden I approached everything as an adventure, a chance to see and do new things. I paid attention to everything around me, soaking it all in—the scenery, the interesting people I met, the new experiences. I didn't know it at the time, but I was planting seeds for my writing career. Eventually, all of those materials would seep into my writing as characters, settings, and story plots.

ARTHUR

Molly certainly did embrace her new life. However, when she asked me if she could go down in the mine, I hesitated. What would the miners think? What would my boss think? And most of all, how would she handle it? Going down into the dark interior of the earth can be a frightening experience.

MOLLY

Arthur led me through the clammy, damp maze of dripping tunnels. The sound echoed off the

Although through most of her married life she had a housekeeper or someone to help with the children, Molly was no stranger to housework. In her book, A Victorian Gentlewoman in the Far West, *when talking about the work she did around the house she wrote, "There was a certain joy in that work too, the satisfaction of perfect success: there is such a thing as a perfect spongecake—I have done pretty well in that line myself—but I never made a perfect drawing. My best work was mere approximation to anything like Art. If to begin was excitement and fresh hope, to finish was disappointment that often verged on despair. But one could always try again."*

rocks, and the miners' voices carried through the cavernous space. The light of a single torch barely pushed back the darkness, and I was constantly aware of the weight of the mountain above me.

HELENA: NEW YORK, SPRING 1877

Molly sent us wonderful letters, brimming with stories and descriptions of her new life. She told me that her landlocked house, perched high up on a lonely ridge, felt like a lighthouse when she stood on her porch and looked out over the ocean of fog in the valley. She described the dry summer heat and the way the afternoon shadows crept toward her cabin as the sun dipped behind great brooding mountains. She delighted in the large fat raindrops that splattered noisily through the trees, sending the scent of damp earth rising like a refreshing cloud.

Naturally, I shared her letters with Richard, my husband and her friend. "She's a good writer," he said folding a letter and tucking it back into the envelope.

DOWN IN THE MINE

Thanks to her own exploration of a mine, the description in Molly's novel, The Led-Horse Claim, *of the heroine's descent into a mine certainly has the ring of truth. "There were far-off, indistinct echoes of life, and subanimate mutterings, the slow respirations of the rocks, drinking air and oozing moisture through their sluggish pores, swelling and pushing against their straightening bonds of timber.... Left to their work, the inevitable forces around her would crush together the sides of the dark galleries and crumble the rough-hewn dome above her head. Cecil did not know the meaning or the power of this inarticulate underground life, but it affected her imagination all the more for her lack of comprehension."*

HIRED HELP

Molly's attitude toward servants was typical of middle-class nineteenth-century America. By 1870, as many as one in eight families employed domestic help. Even during the Foote family's poorest times, Molly always managed to pay for at least one servant, usually more. In Molly's case, however, the presence of household help was truly a necessity. Since she was often the primary breadwinner of the family, it was essential that she have the uninterrupted time she needed to complete her illustrations or write her stories.

RICHARD

Molly was a natural writer. Of course, she needed a little guidance, but what new writer doesn't? When I suggested that she write an article about New Almaden for my magazine, *Scribner's Monthly*, she hesitated, saying, "But I'm an illustrator, not a writer." "Just pretend you are writing a letter," I advised her.

MOLLY: NEW ALMADEN, SPRING 1877

As time passed, I found it frustrating to live in the West and continued to draw pictures of life in the East, so Richard's offer to write and illustrate an article for his magazine came at exactly the right time. I enjoyed the challenge of something new. Besides, it took my mind off my pregnancy and my growing stomach. Although I felt awkward writing, I kept at it.

ARTHUR: APRIL 29, 1877

We welcomed our son, Arthur Burling Foote, into our family with relief and joy. Our house was filling up fast as we had also hired a young woman from back East to help with the baby.

MOLLY

Motherhood took more time than I expected, but, of course, I loved every moment I spent with little Arthur—almost! No matter what I did everyday, thanks to our nanny, I still made time to work on my writing. And true to his word, Arthur never complained or even seemed to mind that I wanted to have both my work and my family.

After I finished the New Almaden article, I hesitated to send it in. "What if Richard hates it?" I asked. "He won't," Arthur reassured me with a smile. So I sent it in, along with strict instructions for Richard to read my work with an unbiased eye. "Forget our friendship," I warned him, and then I waited on pins and needles until I heard back. Richard assured me that the article was perfect for *Scribner's Monthly* and urged me to begin the illustrations. What joy! And what a sight we made when I went out to sketch. The nanny followed me, pushing the baby in his buggy, while I carried my stool and a big white umbrella to keep us in the shade.

WRITTEN AND ILLUSTRATED BY MARY HALLOCK FOOTE

Molly's essay, "A California Mining Camp," appeared in the February 1878 issue of Scribner's Monthly, *accompanied by fourteen of her own illustrations. For both the article and illustrations she received the handsome sum of $300.*

ARTHUR: NEW ALMADEN, AUGUST 1877

And then I quite my job. My relatives thought I was crazy, but Molly understood how I felt. I didn't respect my boss and I couldn't work for a man I didn't respect, no matter what the cost. And there was a cost. Our life was thrown into turmoil. I moved Molly and the baby to a boardinghouse in Santa Cruz, but I was gone so much looking for work and Molly was lonely. Finally, we decided she should take

"A SEA-PORT ON THE PACIFIC"

In the August 1878 edition of Scribner's Monthly, *Molly wrote about her time in Santa Cruz in an article titled, "A Sea-Port on the Pacific."*

It is January, but the air has an Indian summer mildness, with its underlying chill also. The early rains have brought out a tender faint greenness, like a smile over the patient brown hills. The path which we follow along the cliffs toward the town is fringed with budding willows, and a pale, downy-leafed lupine with a dark stem…. As we go down the steps of the bridge, we meet a Chinese washerman shuffling up, with a basket of clean clothes, neatly covered with a sheet, balanced on his shoulder; it is Saturday, and the town is full of them, hurrying in all directions with the weekly wash.

One interesting assignment Molly had during her time in Santa Cruz was to complete a series of illustrations for a story by Louisa May Alcott, appearing in the children's magazine St. Nicholas. The story, along with Molly's illustrations, appeared between December 1877 and October 1878.

the baby and move back to Milton. At least that way she would have her family. And thank goodness she had her illustration and writing work, because most of the time I wasn't making much money.

MOLLY: SPRING 1877–SPRING 1878

I spent the next nineteen months apart from Arthur. I waited for him to find work, worrying that we would never be together again as a family and writing to earn money and fill up my days.

∼ Afterword ∼

ARTHUR FINALLY FOUND WORK AGAIN, this time at a mine in Leadville, Colorado. Molly joined him there in the summer of 1878. They both enjoyed setting up housekeeping, spending time together, meeting new friends, and traveling through the Colorado mountains. Although she spent the winter that year back in Milton, she returned the following spring, eager to settle in and make Leadville their permanent home. Molly's hopes for a home of her own were once again cut short by a miner's strike that put Arthur out of work.

During the next eighteen years, Arthur continued to move from job to job, opportunity to opportunity, while Molly shouldered much of the family's financial responsibility, paying bills with money earned from her writing and drawing. Their family grew by two, Betty born in 1882 and Agnes born in 1886.

As the years passed, Molly no longer accepted commissioned illustration assignments, but instead wrote and illustrated her own work. Despite the family's economic stresses and frequent moves, Molly was a prolific writer and illustrator, and continued to receive glowing reviews for her work.

In 1895, Arthur accepted a job in Grass Valley, California. Finally, Molly, Arthur, and their three children had found a permanent home.

Mary Hallock Foote died on June 25, 1938, at the age of ninety. She left behind a varied legacy. Her illustrations and writing reveal not the Wild West of the cowboy westerns, but instead an educated, domestic West, where families struggled and eventually overcame great odds to survive. Molly Foote left behind more than just stories and illustrations; she left behind the example of a life well lived. In a time when society did not encourage women, much less mothers, to pursue a career, Molly always found a way to create her art. When illustrating scenes of eastern life proved impractical, she turned with equal success to writing about her new life in the West. She supported her husband in his pursuits, while creating a loving and stable home for their three children. Over the course of her career, Molly wrote many books and articles. Her autobiography, *A Victorian Gentlewoman in the Far West*, is still enjoyable reading today and provides a glimpse into the life of a remarkable woman.

⇌ *Bibliography* ⇌

Etulain, Richard W. *Re-imagining the Modern American West: A Century of Fiction, History, and Art.* Tucson, Ariz.: University of Arizona Press, 1996

Foote, Mary Hallock. *A Victorian Gentlewoman in the Far West: The Reminiscences of Mary Hallock Foote.* San Marino, Calif.: The Huntington Library, 1972.

Johnson, Lee Ann. *Mary Hallock Foote.* Boston: Twayne Publishers, 1980.

Larsh, Ed B., and Robert Nichols. *Leadville, U.S.A.* Boulder, Colo.: Johnson Books, 1993.

Miller, Darlis A. *Mary Hallock Foote: Author–Illustrator of the American West.* Norman, Okla.: University of Oklahoma Press, 2002.

Stegner, Wallace. *Angle of Repose.* New York: Penguin Books, 1992.

Once their separation was over, Molly and Arthur enjoyed life in another mountain mining town—this time in Leadville, Colorado. Photograph courtesy of the Denver Public Library Western History Collection.

Helen Hunt Jackson

(1830–1885)

⧽⧼

HELEN HUNT JACKSON was born in 1830, in Amherst, Massachusetts, the oldest of Nathan and Deborah Fiske's two daughters. Right from the start, Helen showed her fiery personality. And although her parents loved her, they didn't quite know how to handle their lively, independent child. "Helen is so wild," Deborah once wrote with concern to a friend.

Helen's happy childhood ended abruptly when her mother died of tuberculosis in 1844. Her father died of the same disease three years later. Helen spent the next few years moving from boarding school to boarding school. A bright, hard-working student, she became a teacher upon graduation and worked until she met Edward Hunt. They married in 1852 and had their first child, Murray, fifteen months later.

The marriage was a happy one, and for a time it seemed that Helen's suffering was behind her. Within two years of her marriage, however, Murray died. Her second son, Rennie, was born a year later, in 1855. In 1863, Edward, a well-respected scientist, was killed unexpectedly while testing out his newest invention, a submarine gun. The ultimate blow came when nine-year-old Rennie died of diphtheria in 1865.

By age 35, Helen had suffered through more loss than most people experience in a lifetime. As a means of easing her terrible grief, she began writing poetry, pouring out her strong emotions into carefully chosen words. On a whim, she signed a poem "Marah," and sent it in to the *New York Evening Post*. That poem, "Keys to the Casket," was published on June 9, 1865.

Helen decided to become a writer and she pursued her goal with single-minded determination. She moved to Newport, Rhode Island, and focused her considerable

OPPOSITE: *Helen Hunt Jackson in 1875. Photograph courtesy of Special Collections, Tutt Library, Colorado College, Colorado Springs.*

energy on learning her newly chosen career. As a result of her hard work and natural talent, Helen soon had established herself with a list of magazines and newspapers that regularly published her writing.

Helen's success came at a price. The long hours spent writing at her desk wore her out. When a constant cough and cold showed no signs of healing, her doctor recommended a trip to Colorado. Helen reluctantly agreed, hoping the clean mountain air might set her on the path to recovery.

HELEN: ON TRAIN TO COLORADO, NOVEMBER 1873

Generally, I loved to travel and had a suitcase always at the ready. But as the train swept west across the dismal, dreary November plains, I felt weak and tired. "Why bother?" I asked myself with more than a little bit of self-pity. But since it is not in my nature to feel sorry for myself, I rested my head against the cool windowpane, closed my eyes, and gave myself a stern talking-to. "You've faced far more difficult trials than this," I told myself. "You've been orphaned, widowed, and have grieved the loss of two children. Starting over in a new town is nothing." I'm happy to say, my little pep talk worked wonders. Soon I was ready to pick up my pencil and describe the scenery that flashed past my window.

Dr. Cates: November 1873

Although dejected about leaving her New England life behind, Helen continued to write. As we rode the train to Colorado, she often picked up her yellow pad and pencil to jot down a stray thought or record an observation. "A pen slows me down," she once told me, and as I watched her write I understood what she meant. Dipping pen into ink was too time-consuming for someone whose hand flew across the page as fast as the train flew across the tracks.

Helen: Colorado Springs, November 1873

Being a single woman without a family or a home, I'd spent the last eight years of my life "making do." Living in boardinghouses, I became an expert at transforming my rented room into a "home" by the creative arrangement of my knickknacks, books, and trinkets. However, when I saw my new residence in Colorado Springs, I feared that for once I might not be up to the task. Imagine moving into a section of town known as Deadman's Row! I learned that the name referred to the many tuberculosis patients who had died there.

Thankfully, an opening soon occurred at the Colorado Springs Hotel, a fairly new establishment and much lauded as the place to be in town. Of course, I moved in immediately.

The rough streets of Colorado Springs were graced with Pikes Peak's majestic beauty. Photograph courtesy of the Denver Public Library Western History Collection.

And then it snowed. The dismal gray sky opened up and lacy white flakes floated down, covering the dusty streets and rough wooden buildings with a cozy blanket of white. My spirits lifted when the sun came out and a field of snow diamonds sparkled outside my window. "Maybe Colorado Springs won't be so bad after all," I told myself, breathing in the fine, fresh air and feeling invigorated by the view from my bedroom of a snow-covered Pikes Peak.

WILLIAM JACKSON: NOVEMBER 1873

A new member joined our friendly little group, a Mrs. Helen Hunt from back east. "She is a famous poet," another guest whispered to me at the dinner table. Of course, I'd never heard of her, but then poetry was not one of my interests. Helen was very small, with brown hair and sparkling eyes. Her bright smile and lively conversation added much to our dinner conversation. I started looking forward to mealtime and made sure business didn't keep me away from the hotel in the evening!

HELEN

Of course, I noticed Mr. Jackson right away. Not only was he handsome, but he also listened so attentively to everything I said. It was really quite flattering if you must know the truth! When he invited me out for a drive to see the scenery, naturally I said yes. I told him that an outing would be good for my health. Although I knew that to be true, I also wanted to get better acquainted with this big, handsome stranger.

WILLIAM

It was still early when I pulled my carriage up to the front door of the hotel. The morning was a chilly fourteen degrees, but Helen didn't mind. Wrapped in furs, she let my high-stepping white horses whisk us away. We drove west. The road wound narrowly up Ute Pass, where a rushing stream bubbled through icy riverbeds and the mountains caught feathery clouds on their snowy peaks. When we stopped, I led Helen out on a rocky ledge and showed her the beauty of the snow-covered valley below. After that first drive, we spent more and more time together, enjoying each other's company.

WILLIAM SHARPLESS JACKSON

At the time when Helen first met William Sharpless Jackson (1836–1919) he was one of the most eligible bachelors in the Colorado Territory. Tall, handsome, and six years younger than Helen, he was a respected and active member of his community. Born a Pennsylvania Quaker, Will began his business career working for the Superior and Mississippi Railroad, a company that built railroad cars. Through perseverance and determination, he worked his way up to the position of company treasurer. William moved west four years before Helen. He eventually became President of the Denver Rio Grande Railroad as well as the founder and president of a Colorado Springs bank.

AMERICA THE BEAUTIFUL

Thirty-four-year-old Katharine Lee Bates visited Colorado in the summer of 1893. She visited many of the local sites, including the grave of Helen Hunt Jackson. One day Miss Bates took a wagon ride over a rough, rutted dirt road to the top of Pikes Peak. Once there, Katharine had only "one brief ecstatic" glimpse of the view before she and the other visitors tumbled back into the wagon and headed down the mountain. In her diary that night, she wrote that the view was "the most glorious scenery I ever beheld," and began to work on the poem that would eventually become the words for the song, "America the Beautiful."

HELEN: COLORADO SPRINGS, SPRING 1874

My health returned and I resumed my vigorous writing schedule. I started early at my desk and worked all morning, ready to stop to eat lunch with William. I began venturing out on my own too, riding a burro I kept at a stable in town. I'm sure I looked a sight, trundling around the mountain roads and trails. I wrote poetry and essays about Colorado and sold them to eastern magazines. Apparently, readers enjoyed my descriptions of the colorful scenery and the sometimes even more colorful characters of the West.

Everything was going smoothly, and then William asked me to marry him. I hesitated. There were so many things to consider. Our ages for one, Will being six years younger than I. And what about our interests? Will's mind was made for business deals and banking, and mine for literature and writing. When I asked him about my writing career, Will reassured me. "I won't interfere," he promised. But deep inside I wondered. Would it bother him to have a wife as devoted to her career as he was to his?

I told Will I needed time to think. "I'll wait," he answered.

WILL: SUMMER 1874

Helen stayed on the go for the rest of that summer, traveling all over Colorado to obtain material for her essays. In the fall, she went east. She said she needed to do all this for her writing career, but I knew better. She was avoiding me and avoiding my question. But I didn't plan on giving up. I bought a fine house on the corner of Kiowa and Weber Streets in Colorado Springs.

An Independent Lady

Helen was a unique woman for her time, and she also had a unique marriage. In an era when women were not expected to be good in business, Helen created a career for herself based not only on her talent as a writer but also on her ability as a businesswoman. Most men from William Jackson's generation would not have found Helen's independence an ideal quality in a wife. Helen's initial worries about her marriage, although sensible, were unfounded. Not only did she continue writing without interference, she also continued to travel when and where she wanted, with or without her husband. Helen and William spent large portions of time apart from each other while pursuing their own careers.

HELEN: NOVEMBER 1874

When I returned to Colorado Springs, Will took me out for a drive and showed me the house. "I bought it for us," he said. No wonder that man was so successful in business—he wouldn't take no for an answer! Finally, I said yes. We agreed to be married the following fall at the house of my sister in Wolfeboro, New Hampshire. For the next year I wrote, traveled, and enjoyed being courted by Will.

CARPENTER: COLORADO SPRINGS, FALL 1875

I worked for Mrs. Jackson, remodeling her house. She sure had a mind of her own, coming every day to look over my shoulder and make sure I did everything exactly as she wanted.

Helen enjoyed living in her newly remodeled house. Photograph courtesy of the Denver Public Library Western History Collection.

IDEAS EVERYWHERE

*L*ike most writers, Helen was always on the lookout for good ideas. And she seemed to find them everywhere she went. For instance, when Helen and Will traveled back east for their wedding, they spent eight days visiting the Philadelphia Centennial Exposition. This exposition featured many of the most interesting and best technological advances of the day. Included in the line up were the largest steam engine ever built and the first public demonstration of Alexander Graham Bell's new-fangled invention, the telephone. Although reluctant to attend, Helen made good use of her time and writing. She sold two articles describing the sights and sounds of the exposition.

THE BUSINESS OF WRITING

*S*ince 1871, a main source of Helen's income had been from the fiction stories she wrote for Scribner's Monthly, *the popular and well-respected national magazine. The stories, written under the pseudonym Saxe Holm, were long and often serialized, or split up over several issues. Helen received $400 for her story, "My Tourmaline," which appeared in four installments between November 1874 and February 1875. This was quite a hefty amount of money for that time period, considering a hard rock miner in nearby Cripple Creek, Colorado, made $3 a day.*

HELEN

Will refused to let me put a bathroom upstairs. Humph! "Who is acting older now?" I teased. He did compromise somewhat by letting me put a water closet in the woodshed. I didn't look forward to those snowy Colorado mornings! Nonetheless, despite our little quarrels, Will let me turn the whole house upside down and inside out.

On Sundays, we took carriage rides up into the mountains, or out on the plains. We carried picnics of cold chicken, fruit, tea, and claret. At night, I read him whatever I'd worked on during the day. He made few comments, but as always served as a good listener.

COLORADO SPRINGS RESIDENT

I must say, for all of her fine words about the beauty and wonders of Colorado, Helen didn't make much of an effort to fit in and know the residents of Colorado Springs. Some gossiped that Mrs. Helen Hunt Jackson thought that she was too good for us, too smart maybe. Others said she was just plain odd. Why I even heard that she arranged her bedroom so that her head faced north when she slept. And we all knew that she didn't attend church. But I thought it was shocking that she admitted it in print, writing that she worshipped God best in nature. And it's true. I saw her many a Sunday morning bouncing along on her burro toward Cheyenne Canyon, when she should have been marching up the front steps of the church.

DR. HOLLAND, EDITOR OF *Scribner's Monthly*: SPRING 1876

Helen sent in her latest story written under her pseudonym, Saxe Holm. We had already published eight of her stories, which readers loved. Helen knew it, too. She attached a note with the manuscript, requesting that we immediately send her the eight hundred dollars of the one thousand eighty dollars that she believed the story was worth. What audacity to not only expect to receive money before a story was published, but to demand a price on top of that! I didn't care if it was Helen Hunt Jackson. I sent that manuscript right back.

HELEN: SPRING 1876

Writing is certainly not for the faint of heart! Dr. Holland's rejection hurt. "Well, I didn't do all that work for nothing," I told myself, and I sat right back down at my desk and tried to

WHO WROTE THAT?

Until the day of her death Helen denied authorship of the Saxe Holm stories published mostly in Scribner's Monthly. *Usually she enjoyed the magazine and newspaper articles that speculated about who Saxe Holm really was; however, she became annoyed when, upon occasion, someone would publicly proclaim responsibility for her work.*

CHECK, PLEASE

There is no doubt that Helen wrote to make money. She depended on the money she earned. In those days, making money wasn't considered ladylike behavior, but Helen knew better. Once she wrote in a letter to the editor of The Atlantic, *"Cash is a vile article, but there is one thing viler, and that is a purse without any cash in it."*

figure out what else I could do with that story. I remembered that another editor, Thomas Niles of Roberts Brothers in Boston, was publishing a "No Name" book series in which well-known authors write books without signing their names. "What a clever idea," I thought, when he explained it to me. The editor knew that aside from being drawn to the story, just plain curiosity would entice readers to open each book and try their hand at guessing the author. I contacted Mr. Niles and asked if I could submit a book manuscript to him for this series. Of course, he readily agreed, so I began the rather arduous process of turning an eighty-page magazine story into a two hundred-page book.

HELEN: BOSTON, LATE SUMMER 1878

I packed my trunks and arranged my writing supplies for a trip to Boston, eager to leave Colorado. My publisher in Boston needed my help selecting poems for a new book. I was delighted to have an excuse to leave Colorado Springs as I missed my writing friends.

When I arrived, Boston was all atwitter. Everyone was talking about the small group of Ponca Indians who were booking lecture halls and giving speeches about the terrible treatment they had received from the U.S. government. Of course, I went to see for myself what all the fuss was about.

Chief Standing Bear and his beautiful young interpreter, Bright Eyes, told their story in the hopes of raising sympathy and money for their cause. And what a story! I sat absolutely mesmerized from the minute the lights went out.

The Ponca Indians lived and farmed peacefully on their reservation in the Dakota Territory until 1868, at which time the U.S. government mistakenly included some of the Ponca's land in a reservation they gave to the Sioux. The Poncas didn't move off their land, and so, in 1876, the government demanded that they relocate to Indian Territory. Of course, the Poncas did not want to leave their homes and their farms, but the government insisted, reassuring them that if they didn't like the new land they could come back.

CHIEF STANDING BEAR: FALL 1879

Ten chiefs traveled with an agent to Indian Territory. We saw the land the government wanted to give us. It was useless land. Leftover land. Land that couldn't be farmed. We said, "No."

The Indian Agent left us there in that new land with no money and unable to speak the white man's language.

The government forced my people to move. Have you ever watched your loved ones suffer and die? That year, one hundred sixty of my people died from disease, poverty, and starvation. My own son was among them. I left the Indian Territory. Others came with me. We walked for three months until Chief Joseph welcomed us onto the Omaha Reservation, our feet bloody and our bodies weak.

THE PONCA

The Ponca were a Plains Indian tribe who lived in Northeastern Nebraska along the rich lowlands of the Missouri River Valley. They divided their time between hunting buffalo and farming crops of corn, beans, and tobacco. The Ponca were a peaceful people, and as Helen pointed out in a December 14, 1979, editorial in the New York Evening Post, they never fought or killed any U.S. soldiers, even when they were being removed at gunpoint from their homes.

CARL SCHURZ

Carl Schurz (1829–1906) moved to the United States from his native Germany in 1852 at twenty-three years of age. He became a member of the Republican Party and found work at the Tribune as a Washington correspondent. Stepping into the political arena, he served as Missouri's senator. In 1877, he was appointed Secretary of the Interior by President Rutherford B. Hayes. Although it was Schurz's predecessor who actually made the order against the Ponca Indians, Schurz did nothing to correct or rescind the order.

Soldiers arrested us. They said we left Indian Territory without permission.

The government lied to me. They took my land. They killed my son. And then they put me in jail.

Helen

That wasn't the end of Standing Bear's story. General Crook, under orders from Carl Schurz, the new Secretary of the Interior, arrested Standing Bear. But Crook felt bad about the arrest and contacted his friend Thomas Tibbles, the assistant editor of the *Omaha Tribune*. Together Tibbles and Crook found a lawyer who agreed to help Standing Bear. The lawyer put his case before a judge in Nebraska, who decided that Standing Bear had the right to present his case to the Supreme Court. Standing Bear was freed from jail.

Bright Eyes

I am from the Omaha tribe, but we are friends and family with the Ponca. I traveled with Chief Standing Bear to Boston to help him tell his story. For me, it was an honor and a duty to help my people. Chief Standing Bear's story is the story of all Indians.

Thomas Henry Tibbles and Bright Eyes

In her book, The Indian Reform Letters of Helen Hunt Jackson, 1879–1885, *editor Valerie Sherer Mathes wrote a brief biography of Thomas Henry Tibbles (1838–1928) saying he "was an itinerant Methodist preacher before becoming a reporter on the* Omaha Daily Bee *and later on the* Omaha Daily Herald. *In 1881, he married Bright Eyes or Susette La Flesche, an Omaha Indian woman who had served as Standing Bear's interpreter."*

Of Helen, Tibbles wrote in his memoir, Buckskin and Blanket Days, *that she threw "every ounce of her own strong influence into the scale in dealing with members of Congress, senators, editors, and writers."*

HELEN

The story of the Poncas touched me deeply. Something inside me said, "You must help." That very night I put pen to paper. I wrote out Standing Bear's account for the *Independent*, a New York weekly newspaper that regularly bought my poems and essays. I signed the article "Justice." It made me feel good that my writing might help someone else.

INTERIOR SECRETARY SCHURZ

Helen Hunt Jackson was a thorn in my side. With her poisonous pen, she wrote essays and letters for the newspapers, trying to get sympathy for the Poncas. Ha! Doesn't that woman know Indians have no rights?

I ignored her at first. But her persistence left me no choice, so I decided I, too, could use the power of public opinion. I wrote a letter explaining my side of the situation. The *New York Tribune* printed my letter. I thought that would take care of the situation, but it didn't. Lo and behold, that troublesome woman answered me with another essay. She shot down all of my explanations and then asked for more.

HELEN: NEW YORK, WINTER 1879

At first I thought I would write one or two articles to help the Poncas. But when I started my research, I came across story after story that revealed the government's lies and deceit. Hunched over stacks of documents in New York City's Astor Library, I felt like a detective, looking for clues, sorting through facts and figures. The more I read, the angrier I became. Each new piece of information drove me to

PSEUDONYMS

Pseudonyms are names that authors make up and sign to their work to hide the true authorship of a piece. Rip Van Winkle, Justice, Marah and Saxe Holm are a few of the pseudonyms Helen signed during her writing career. Probably one reason she sought anonymity in her writing was that much of the reading public was hostile to women writers, believing that it wasn't proper for women to show their intellect or air their opinions so openly.

BLOCKHEAD

Schurz replied to Helen's accusations in a public letter printed in the December 19, 1879, issue of the Tribune. *His rebuttal was titled, "Mr. Schurz on Indian Affairs: The Secretary Replied to the Letter of H.H. in the* Tribune." *After reading his public reply, Helen gleefully wrote a friend: "Is the man a blockhead? Does he suppose he has helped his cause?"*

Even experienced writers, such as Helen, felt the need to revise, as this rough draft page from her book Ramona *clearly shows. Photograph courtesy of Special Collections, Tutt Library, Colorado College, Colorado Springs.*

write more. And each day, I left my desk filled with sorrow over the injustices suffered by an innocent people.

WILL: EARLY SPRING 1880

Helen spent day after day, week after week scribbling away in a study alcove of the library. She said it was her duty to inform the American people. "Calm down," I wrote her, as she got more and more riled over what she called her "Indian problem." Helen's strong feelings lead her into action, and I worried about her. She was creating a stir with her writing, but she was also making enemies. It was bad enough when she wrote about the problem of the Ponca Indians from Nebraska. But then she started writing about the situations with other Indian tribes, including the Colorado Utes. Colorado residents did not like what she said about our state.

HELEN: NEW YORK, EARLY SPRING 1880

One day, I woke up with the phrase "A Century of Dishonor" ringing in my head. I was still half asleep, yet I knew at that moment that I would write a book about the government's dastardly treatment of the Indians. I knew just the way I would approach it, too. Quoting from public documents, I would let the government tell

A DRAMATIC INTRODUCTION

In her book, Helen Hunt Jackson: A Lonely Voice of Conscience, *Antoinette May wrote that after* A Century of Dishonor *was published, she "sent a copy at her own expense to every member of Congress. Printed in red on the cover were the words of Benjamin Franklin: 'Look upon your hands! They are stained with the blood of your relations.'"*

their own dishonorable story. I worked feverishly. The words flowed so fast from my pen that my hand could barely keep up. I wrote thousands of words each day and completed the book in May 1880.

～ *Afterword* ～

HELEN'S FIGHT FOR the Indians did not stop with the publishing of her book, *A Century of Dishonor*. In fact, that was just the beginning.

Disappointed in the public's response or, more correctly, lack of response to her book, she thought that another way to gain public sympathy for the Indians was to do what Harriet Beecher Stowe had already done for the slaves with her book *Uncle Tom's Cabin*. In other words, tell a story. She thought that maybe, as readers began to sympathize with the Indians in the story, they might begin to sympathize with Indians in real life.

Based on real-life events, Helen started her book, *Ramona*, on December 1, 1883. And just as in *A Century of Dishonor*, the words and the story poured out of her. She worked continuously until the book was completed on March 8, 1884.

Upon completion of *Ramona*, Helen returned home to Colorado for much-needed rest. Unfortunately, while there she fell down the stairs and broke her hip. In her weakened condition, she became sick with a long-lasting cold and cough. She traveled to California in hopes that the warm air would help her recover. Instead, her condition gradually worsened until she was confined to her bed. Still, she continued her letter-writing campaign for the Indian cause up until the day of her death on August 8, 1885.

A few weeks before she died, Helen wrote to a friend, "My *Century of Dishonor* and *Ramona* are the only things I have done of which I am glad. The rest is of no moment. They will live and they will bear fruit."

A DIFFERENT APPROACH

Helen was surprised that she approached the writing of her book, A Century of Dishonor, *differently than the way she ordinarily wrote. In a letter to her husband, she explained, "I write these sentences—which would ordinarily cost me much thought and work, to get them so condensed—as fast as I can write the words."*

≈ *Bibliography* ≈

Banning, Evelyn I. *Helen Hunt Jackson: A Lonely Voice of Conscience.* New York: The Vanguard Press, 1973.

Jackson, Helen Hunt. *A Century of Dishonor.* Norman, Okla.: University of Oklahoma Press, 1995.

———. *Ramona.* New York: Signet Classics, 2002.

Mathes, Valerie Sherer, ed. *The Indian Reform Letters of Helen Hunt Jackson, 1879–1885.* Norman, Okla.: University of Oklahoma Press, 1998.

May, Antoinette. *Helen Hunt Jackson: A Lonely Voice of Conscience.* San Francisco: Chronicle Books, 1987.

O'Dell, Ruth. *Helen Hunt Jackson.* New York: D. Appleton-Century Co., 1939.

Pierce-Griffin, Trudy. *The Encyclopedia of Native America.* New York: Viking, 1995.

West, Mark I., ed. *Bits of Colorado: Helen Hunt Jackson's Writings for Readers.* Palmer Lake, Colo.: Filter Press, 2000.

———. *Westward to a High Mountain: The Colorado Writings of Helen Hunt Jackson.* Denver, Colo.: Colorado Historical Society, 1994.

Wolfson, Evelyn. *From Abenaki to Zuni: A Dictionary of Native American Tribes.* New York: Walker and Co., 1988.

Gertrude Simmons Bonnin

(1876–1938)

⨭⨴⨵

G ERTRUDE SIMMONS BONNIN was a member of the Yankton Sioux tribe. Born to a Sioux mother and a white father, she never lived with her father and never really knew him. As a little girl, Gertrude lived with her mother, Ellen Simmons or Taté Iyóhiwin, on the Yankton Reservation in what is now the southeast corner of South Dakota. Fighting the white man's influence in their daily lives, Taté Iyóhiwin worked hard to raise Gertrude in the traditional Sioux lifestyle. Gertrude spoke her native tongue and learned the practical skills of gathering and preparing food. She was taught about her heritage and history through the tradition of storytelling.

THE YANKTON SIOUX

T *he Sioux are part of the larger cultural group known as Plains Indians. Generally, these Indians lived a nomadic life of hunting and gathering. The Cheyenne, the Arapaho, the Mandan, and the Comanche are just a few Plains Indian tribes.*

The Sioux consists of thirteen individual tribes. For many years, their territory covered the land in the upper Mississippi River Valley to the Black Hills area of what is now western South Dakota. Gertrude's people, the Yankton Sioux, had a long and peaceful history with the white man. They met trappers and traders as early as the late 1700s. Lewis and Clark stayed at a Yankton village on their great expedition (see sidebar on page 68), and the first wave of white settlers encroached on their land in the mid-1800s.

OPPOSITE: *As an adult, Gertrude called herself Zitkala-Sä in order to honor her Sioux heritage. Reproduced by permission from the Collections of the Library of Congress.*

Although she had adult brothers and sisters, Gertrude lived alone with her mother. Her brother, David, who was nine years older, left for an Indian boarding school when Gertrude was a small girl. He didn't return until Gertrude herself was about to leave for an Indian school in Indiana.

GERTRUDE: YANKTON RESERVATION, SOUTH DAKOTA, SUMMER 1883

Walking through the tall prairie grass, my mother and I startled a quail out of its hiding place. As the bird rose into the air, I followed it, running as fast as my uncle's pony. Mother laughed to see one wild thing chasing another. But when I turned around, breathless and windblown, I saw her face darken briefly, like the prairie does when a cloud passes over the sun. Even though I was little, I knew a shadowed memory had passed through her mind. And although she didn't cry, I sensed her sadness.

TATÉ IYÓHIWIN, GERTRUDE'S MOTHER

Gertrude was a happy child—wild, with a spirit as big as a cloudless sky. She didn't mind living on the reservation because she knew nothing else. Sometimes though, when I saw her run so freely across the prairie, I couldn't help but think of another daughter, who had died many years before when our people, the Yankton Sioux, had been herded like cattle away from our homeland. Although Gertrude's lively spirit made my heart sing, it also worried me. She didn't know the complete freedom and joy of living in a land without the white man. I worried that contact with the non–Indian way of life would destroy her spirit the way that it had destroyed mine.

SIOUX VILLAGE

Although members of the Yankton tribe lived on the Yankton reservation, the tribe was actually divided into eight small bands spread out across the entire reservation. Each band lived together in circular camps of tipis. Before the days of the reservation, the band needed to be large enough to form a hunting party, but not so large that they could not pack up their camps and move quickly. Although these bands of Yankton Sioux lived separately from each other, they generally gathered together several times a year for religious ceremonies. Tradition prevented young people from marrying within their own band, and when a man married, he usually went to live with his wife's band.

GERTRUDE

I lived in a circular village of tipis. Besides my mother, there were always aunts and uncles to teach me, cousins to play with, and elders to share their stories. I spent hours playing with my two best friends, Thowin and Judéwin. We particularly liked to play a game called "pretend grownup." We would sit with knees bent around a make-believe fire, pretending to prepare and cook our food. "Han! Han! Yes! Yes!" we would say to each other's made-up stories of warrior husbands. Clucking over fussy children and admiring our beautiful hand-beaded clothing, we sounded so much like our mothers that soon our game dissolved into laughter.

Our parents often urged us to go out onto the rolling prairie, where we chased cloud shadows and played hide-and-seek in the tall grass. When our stomachs growled with hunger, we used sharp digging sticks to uncover sweet roots to eat. When our skin felt hot and sticky, we splashed and played in the river.

After an exhausting day of play, I always felt a sense of peace when I crested the hill to return to my village. Sometimes I rested on top of that hill, lying on my stomach to watch the

GAMES CHILDREN PLAY

In his book, Daily Life in a Plains Indian Village 1868, *Michael 'Bad Hand' Terry said that, "Plains Indian children's games are often an imitation of the roles that they will play as adults. Boys play at war and hunting, and girls play dollhouse with miniature tipis and dolls made out of sticks and scraps of cloth. Both boys and girls play ball and stick games similar to hockey or lacrosse, which are also enjoyed by adults."*

activity of the camp just like I watched the activity of the large anthills I found on the prairie. I saw my mother bending over the cooking pot, while my aunt sewed a pair of moccasins for my cousin Wahċáziwin (Yellow Flower Woman). A white-haired elder sat in the shade, smoking his pipe, and gently scolded a child who chased a puppy too close to the fire, while a brave rode in slowly from the opposite direction with his day's hunt slung over his horse. Finally, my mother's voice and the smell of the evening meal floated up to call me home.

GERTRUDE'S AUNT: FALL 1873

It is the way of our people that children prepare for adulthood by helping their parents with the work. As the summer cooled to autumn, Gertrude, her mother, and I busied ourselves with preparations for winter. We husked and shelled the corn. When we set it out on a blanket to dry in the sun, Gertrude shooed away the crows, squirrels, and chipmunks. When Taté Iyóhiwin cut the pumpkin into flat, circular pieces, Gertrude strung them like beads and hung them from a pole to dry in the sun and wind. We all enjoyed leaving camp early to collect the wild fruit that grew on the prairie, while the cool mist of the morning still clung to the ground, and our moccasins left trails through the dewy grass. We walked great distances to gather wild plums or sweet red raspberries. Gertrude kept us laughing with her cheerful chatter.

GERTRUDE

I liked learning the ways of a Sioux woman. I enjoyed working with my aunt, who laughed out loud and teased a smile onto my mother's solemn face. Working together was more fun than playing "pretend grown-ups" with my friends. I looked forward to doing these chores for my own family.

Gertrude felt safe and loved, growing up amidst a typical Sioux Village. Illustration courtesy of the Denver Public Library Western History Collection.

TATÉ IYÓHIWIN

Gertrude learned to bead by watching me, and it quickly became one of her favorite occupations. Usually a bundle of energy, she sat quietly beside me on the sunny side of the tipi as I laid out my work and arranged the different colors of beads in puddles around me. After she had watched me for awhile, I gave her an awl and a piece of soft leather.

GERTRUDE

My mother was gentle but also strict. When I first created my own beadwork designs, they had too many colors and intricate details. When the work got hard, I cried and wanted to quit. "No, you must finish what you start," my mother said firmly. I soon learned to make simple designs with pleasing colors, and I enjoyed my work. When I was done, however, I often shot away from the tipi like an arrow fired from a bow, calling to my friends on the fly.

TATÉ IYÓHIWIN

Once a month, I took Gertrude's hand and we walked over the prairie hills until we came to the road, one of the white man's dusty scars cutting across our land.

GREENWOOD, SOUTH DAKOTA

Greenwood was a bustling town. Once an Indian agency was established there to manage the reservation and hand out the rations, a whole community of white workers and their families followed. The Reservation Agency headquarters was set up along Greenwood's main street, as well as some houses for the employees, a blacksmith shop, a few general stores run by merchants with government licenses, two trading posts, a barbershop, and a livery stable. On another street running next to the Missouri River were warehouses that stored the rations being handed out, as well as supplies used by the agency. There was also a three-story hotel that usually boarded steamboat travelers chugging up and down the Missouri River.

We followed that road down into the town of Greenwood to claim our monthly ration of food. Standing in line outside the Indian agency, we often waited until our feet ached and the sun had traveled across the sky. I did not want to take anything from the white man. I did not want to dirty my moccasins with the mud and dust from his town. But what choice did I have? My people, the Sioux, had paid for this food with our land. Sometimes we waited in line for hours, only to be turned away empty handed. "Go home," the agent ordered us. "There is no more food left," he said with a cruel smile.

SHARING

A deeply held value of the Sioux culture was the act of sharing. This was often seen in a ceremony they called the Give-Away. Hosted by a single person or group of people, it was meant to celebrate a birthday, special occasion, or heroic act. During the festivities, the host gave away presents, such as farm equipment, blankets, and handmade beadwork to all the guests, with the most valuable gifts going to the most honored guests.

INDIAN AGENT

Of course, there was no more food left. I had sold it. The owner of the restaurant in town had white customers to feed. I'd say that was more important than a bunch of begging Indians. "It's rancid meat," I warned him, but he bought it anyway. In return, I put a nice fat wad of money into my own pocket. Of course, this little deal was done without the government's knowledge, if you know what I mean. The two of us laughed when we saw those Indians standing in line to claim what I had already given away. Anyway, they should feel lucky to get whatever food I decide to give

Much like Gertrude did with her mother, these Sioux Indians are waiting for supplies at the Pine Ridge Reservation in South Dakota. Photograph courtesy of the Denver Public Library Western History Collection.

them. After all, beggars can't be choosers, I always say. So what if I sell some of the food that the United States government sent to them? Do you think the government cares? Well, they don't. The Indians aren't even U.S. citizens.

PAID IN FULL

In the 1880s, Indians on reservations across the United States were often perceived as beggars who lived on handouts. In truth, the rations they were supposed to receive, but often didn't, were bought and paid for with their tribal land and resources. In the case of the Yankton Sioux, Struck-by-the-Ree signed an 1858 treaty that gave away eleven million acres of land in exchange for 430,000 acres of "reserved" or protected land. The federal government also promised to supply food, lumber, farming equipment, cash and other services totaling 1.6 million dollars over the next fifty years. In constantly cheating the Indians out of their already paid-for land, food, and supplies, it was not the Indians but the U.S. government that did not uphold their end of the bargain.

GERTRUDE

As we walked up Greenwood's main street on issue days, I peeked inside the general store. Nothing fascinated me more than the colorful rows of tin cans that lined the shelves. "How does the white man get that food inside those little cans?" I asked my mother. She just shrugged.

From the government we received, if we were lucky, beef, flour, sugar, salt, and coffee. But that wasn't all we ate. We gathered the food that Mother Earth provided. Sometimes the men left the reservation without permission to hunt for deer, but often they only came back with rabbits or squirrels. The women searched for eggs hidden in nests in the long swamp grass at the edge of the river. My mouth watered as I smelled the sharp tang of wild onions when I pulled them from the ground, thinking of the stew my mother would make that night.

TATÉ IYÓHIWIN

When we had enough food, I wanted to share it with others in our camp. Often the elders had even less than we did. That was the way of our people. We shared our food, our belongings, and our labor with each other.

GERTRUDE

Many a late afternoon, as my mother cut up the meat and vegetables and dumped them into the big black pot that hung over the fire, she would send me to another tipi to invite a relative or friend to share our evening meal. "Wait until they speak to you," she always said before I left. So I waited politely outside the tipi, waiting for them to

LISTEN AND LEARN

Without a written language, one of the primary ways the Sioux educated their children was through winter storytelling. Legends and traditional stories were a way through which Yankton elders taught children the values and history of the tribe. The same stories were told over and over again so that the children memorized them. The elders also told stories and legends that explained the Indian's relationship to the natural world and the spiritual world. As a young adult, Gertrude wrote a book for children, Old Indian Legends, in which she took some of the stories she loved as a child and put them down on paper. Gertrude wanted to teach non-Indian children about the dignity and beauty of her culture.

notice me. "What is it, my grandchild?" the elder would say and the invitation poured from my mouth. During dinner, I sat silently by my mother's side as the adult conversation swirled around me, the words darting in and out of my head like a bumblebee around a flower. For these words, I did not care and closed my ears. When everyone was finished eating, my mother put another log on the fire. Firelight flickered on the faces around the circle. As the elder wove words together to tell stories, I snuggled into the warm softness of a buffalo robe. Outside we could hear the distant howl of a wolf, but inside the tipi felt warm and safe.

INDIAN AGENT

Part of my job was to keep an eye on all of the Indians on the Yankton Reservation. They lived in eight villages spread out over the prairie and I would ride out to check on them. Doggone it! Those Indians sure made me nervous. No telling what they might be planning to do. The government wanted me to keep the peace and one sure way of doing that was to keep all of those Indians apart. If they lived on small farms, the way the U.S. government wanted them to, they would be separate from each other and couldn't get themselves into trouble, especially with those religious ceremonies they have. All that dancing and singing around their campfires was sure to stir them up. No wonder the government didn't like them to practice their religion. It's dangerous.

TATÉ IYÓHIWIN: WINTER 1883–1884

One sparkling winter morning, as the sun threw diamonds across the snow, my worst fears came true. Some Quaker missionaries came to our village looking for students for their school. My son, David, had already been to an Indian school. He left our village a Sioux and came back acting like the son of a white man,

DIVIDE TO CONQUER

As Doreen Rappaport explains in her book, The Flight of Red Bird: The Life of Zitkala-Sä, the government wanted to "Destroy tribal unity and traditional life by breaking up the social units, by moving people from their tipi villages to houses scattered across the reservation." One might wonder the purpose of this, and the answer is complex, but includes the fact that the government thought that the Indians would be easier to control. They also felt that white culture was superior to Native American culture. Much of it boils down, however, to greed. The white man wanted the land, water, and resources controlled by the Indians.

First Indian School

The first school for Indians, Carlisle Indian School, funded by the U.S. government, was founded in 1879 by Richard Henry Pratt, a captain in the United States Army. He first got the idea for the school when, as an army officer and Indian fighter, he noticed that a group of Indian prisoners at Fort Marion in St. Augustine, Florida, were so unhappy that they began to sicken and die. Pratt decided something must be done immediately. He organized the Indians into army-like companies and appointed a few as officers in charge of the others. He invited local white people to visit the prison and read and teach English to the Indians. Soon, the Indians' morale improved, and they became model prisoners. One visitor to the prison was Harriet Beecher Stowe, author of the famous book about slavery, Uncle Tom's Cabin.

"Kill the Indian"

Captain Pratt believed that in order to "civilize" the Native Americans of the West, it was necessary to "Kill the Indian in him and save the man." The whole premise of the Indian school system was to remove the Indian child from his parents and village, thus removing him from the Indian culture, values, language, and beliefs that shaped him. By 1884, the year that Gertrude went to White's Manual Labor Institute, there were forty-nine Indian boarding schools set up across the country.

dressed in his suit, his short hair combed to the side, speaking English with his friends. Now the missionaries wanted to take Gertrude to their school.

David

I had only been home from school for a short time. When the white men came and asked about Gertrude, I mumbled an answer and hurried over to discuss this with my mother. I told her not to send Gertrude to an Indian school. Although I've chosen many of the white man's ways, I'll never forget the pain of those first months away from home.

Gertrude

The Quaker missionaries rumbled up to our village in a wagon. My mother ordered me to stay away from them, but my friend Judéwin told me how the missionaries brought presents to her tipi and shared stories of their beautiful faraway land. They promised her a ride on the iron horse if she agreed to come to their school. I wanted presents. I wanted to ride on the iron horse. "Just listen to them," I begged my mother over and over again.

Taté Iyóhiwin

"They have fooled you with their lies, my child," I said sadly, but I allowed them to enter my tipi.

Gertrude

Mother said the missionaries were cruel, but when they spoke to me their words were soft and comfortable, their gestures were gentle, and their eyes smiled when they patted me on the head.

When they left I cried, begging my mother over and over to let me go with them to their school. I closed my ears to her words of warning and closed my eyes to the look of sadness and fear in her face. Finally, my mother said yes to the missionaries.

Taté Iyóhiwin

Gertrude thought the decision about school was up to me, but I knew the truth, that I had no choice. Sometimes the missionaries stole Indian children from their homes if their parents refused. Or the Indian agent cut off the rations to the whole family, slowly starving them into agreement. I knew that eventually Gertrude would leave me and I thought if she wanted to go, it would be easier for her. Besides, more and more white men were coming into our land. She needed to learn the white man's language, to understand his culture in order to survive.

Spotted Tail

In order to get the first class of children to come to his school, Pratt visited a group of Sioux Indians. At the Rosebud Reservation in South Dakota, he gathered together forty warriors and chiefs and presented the idea of a school where Indian children would come to learn the white man's language and letters. At first, Spotted Tail, a respected chief, responded by saying, "The white people are all thieves and liars. We do not want our children to learn such things." He complained about how the white man's government had taken away Indian land and had not honored their treaties. Pratt listened politely and then explained that Spotted Tail was cheated because he did not understand the white man's language or read the white man's words. Pratt reasoned that if Spotted Tail's children knew this language, they would be able to negotiate better deals. After much discussion, the Indian chiefs agreed to send their children to the Carlisle School for Indians.

Gertrude

Several days later, wrapped in heavy blankets to keep out the cold, my mother and I walked to the missionaries' waiting carriage. There were dark shadows under her eyes, and she held my hand tightly until I broke free and raced ahead, eager to see my friends. We greeted each other with shouts and giggles, three boys, two older girls, and me and my two best friends. I proudly showed them the brand new moccasins my mother had made for me.

Missionary

The children climbed into the carriage and we drove away to catch the train. I saw the pain in the mothers' eyes, but I ignored it. I knew in my heart that we were right. We might be breaking their hearts, but we were saving the souls of their heathen children.

Gertrude: White's Manual Labor Institute, Wabash Indiana, March 1884

The missionaries changed once we got on the train. A tone of impatience crept into their voices when they directed us to our seats. Their eyes no longer smiled. I huddled in the corner of the train bench, suddenly silent and afraid.

For several days our train rattled east. At first, the sights racing by our window were familiar, but then we passed through towns and frozen fields. A little white girl, shorter than me, pointed at us. She spoke words that we did not understand, but her face looked like she had eaten a rotten piece of meat. When we walked by, her mother stepped aside, so as not to touch us.

We reached the grounds of our school, White's Manual Labor Institute, at night. Even

TRAIN RIDE

"I sat perfectly still, with my eyes downcast, daring only now and then to shoot long glances around me. Chancing to turn to the window at my side, I was quite breathless upon seeing one familiar object. It was the telegraph pole which strode by in short paces. Very near my mother's dwelling, along the edge of a road thickly bordered with wild sunflowers, some poles like these had been planted by white men. Often I had stopped, on my way down the road, to hold my ear against the pole, and, hearing its low moaning, I used to wonder what the pale-face had done to hurt it. Now I sat watching for each pole that glided by to be the last one."

—From an article by Gertrude Bonnin: "Impressions of an Indian Childhood"
(*Atlantic Monthly*, Vol. 85, January 1900)

though I was tired, my fear kept me wide awake as a tall brick building loomed up before us. Yellow light came from the windows and fell like square blocks on the snow-covered lawn. When the women led us in, the brightness hurt my eyes. It wasn't like the warm glow of the campfire.

RED-FACED TEACHER

My heart hurt for the Indian children as they shuffled into the front hall and then cowered against the cold brick wall. When I first saw Gertrude, she stared out at me from within her blanket cocoon. Brown eyes followed my every movement and widened in surprise when I lifted her up in my arms to comfort her. Her body stiffened. I jiggled her up and down, trying to sound jolly and happy, trying to express through my tone that she was welcome here. She looked angrily at me and the flash of her eyes let me know better than any words that she wanted to be let down, and instantly. "Good for you," I said to her. I knew that she would need a tough spirit to survive the changes ahead.

GERTRUDE

They led us into a big room with many tables. The red-faced woman motioned to the chairs, pulling one out so its claws scraped loudly against the wooden floor. When they put some food in front of us, I couldn't choke it down past the lump in my throat.

More about White's Manual Labor Institute

Like Carlisle before it, White's was set up to run like a military school. The day was divided into a strict schedule, and the children were called to their tasks by a system of bells and whistles. The students not only attended classes, but spent much time doing the actual work of running the school. The boys worked in the fields to help grow the food that they ate, while the girls worked in the kitchen, did the laundry, and attended to cleaning the building. This system not only made it cheaper to run the school, it provided on-the-job training for the children, who were then expected to have the skills necessary to leave the school and run their own farms and keep their own houses.

No Turning Back

What the missionaries didn't explain to Gertrude and her friends was that once she arrived at White's, she was stuck there until her three-year course of studies was through. The children were not allowed to go home, even for summer vacation. School officials feared that their students might never come back, and if they did, all their hard work of winning them away from the Indian way would have been undone. As a consequence, many children suffered so severely from homesickness that they actually became physically sick. Some even died.

Red-faced Teacher

While she ate, Gertrude started chattering in her own language, making the same sounds over and over again and pointing frantically toward the door. I didn't know what she was trying to tell me, but I suspect she wanted to go home. Of course she did. They all do at first.

Gertrude

The red-faced woman smiled sadly, patted me on the head and then led me upstairs to a room with many beds. She placed her head on her clasped hands and closed her eyes. After a brief moment, she motioned for me to lie down and do the same. When I did, she left the room and turned out the light. I began to cry with great heaving sobs.

The next morning, my clothes and moccasins were gone and in their place they gave me the clothing of a white girl. Judéwin and I looked at each other shyly as we fingered our new dresses. The teacher ladies rushed in and dressed us right away in these new uncomfortable and confining dresses. The buttons confused my fingers and the shoes pinched my feet and hurt when I walked.

ADJUSTMENT

"A loud-clamoring bell awakened us at half past six in the cold winter mornings. From happy dreams of Western rolling lands and unlassoed freedom we tumbled out upon chilly bare floors back again into a paleface day. We had short time to jump into our shoes and clothes, and wet our eyes with icy water, before a small hand bell was vigorously rung for roll call."

—From Gertrude Bonnin's "The School Days of an Indian Girl"
(*Atlantic Monthly*, Vol. 85, February 1900)

JUDÉWIN

I already knew a few words of English, and the next morning I overheard some of the teachers talking about us. "We will cut their hair," they said. I don't know why this surprised me since everyone around us had hair chopped short, but in our culture women only cut their hair short as a sign that they were in mourning. And to have shingled or layered hair was the sign of a coward. Shaking with fear and apprehension, I confided my secret to Gertrude, who, of course, replied that she would not let them. "They are stronger and older than us," I warned.

GERTRUDE

"I will not submit," I said to Judéwin. "I will show them that I'm not a coward." And so as soon as I saw a chance I took it. Sneaking away from the group, I wandered around the big building in search of a place to hide. I poked my head in cupboards and looked into closets. Upstairs I found a darkened room with three beds lined up against the wall. I crawled under one of the beds and shrank into the corner, trying to make myself as small and invisible as I could. I imagined myself a little mouse hiding in its burrow as the eagle swoops above. And just like

NEW LANGUAGE, NEW THOUGHTS

One of the goals of the Indian schools was to have the Indian children replace their native language with English. Changing their language was yet another way to influence their thoughts. In his book, Indian School: Teaching the White Man's Way, *Michael L. Cooper quotes a young Arapaho girl from Carlisle who explains this point.* "Hours, minutes, and seconds were such small divisions of time that we had never thought of them. When the sun rose, when it was high in the sky, and when it set were all the divisions of the day that we had ever found necessary when we followed the old Arapaho road. When we went on the hunting trip or to a sun dance, we counted time by sleeps."

that mouse I saw feet and legs running by, and the ground shook from the weight. "I will show them that I am not a coward," I vowed again to myself.

JUDÉWIN

When the teachers couldn't find Gertrude, they looked angry. They made me look for her and call her name. I called quietly because in my heart I wanted Gertrude to escape.

GERTRUDE

Tap. Tap. Tap. Hard shoes hit the wooden floor as people rushed by in the hallway. I remained silent, even when I heard Judéwin call my name. "No one will cut my hair," I whispered.

White-haired Teacher

I found Gertrude hiding like an animal under a bed. Well, you can believe that I grabbed her ankles and dragged her out into the daylight. She kicked and screamed and fought like the dickens, and I had the scratch marks to prove it. But I was used to the ways of these wild children. That little girl carried on so, why you'd think we were hurting her. Didn't she know that she should be grateful we are cleaning her up, giving her some decent clothing and putting a full plate in front of her?

Gertrude

That was the morning of my first day in school. It took a long time for that place to feel safe or comfortable. But as I learned the white man's language and eventually learned to read the white man's papers, I found out that I was a good student. I made friends and was happy there. I missed my mother and living at home, but I loved learning and I loved writing and reading.

> ## General Allotment Act
>
> The year Gertrude returned from White's was the year U.S. Congress passed the General Allotment Act. Each Indian in every western reservation was to receive a parcel of 160 acres to be used as an individual farm. As a consequence, this freed up even more land for white settlers as the government went on to sell the left-over reservation land to non–Indians.

After three years I returned home. At eleven years old, I was no longer an Indian, but I was not a white person either. I didn't know what to do or how to act. What clothes do I wear? How do I fix my hair? I missed learning and reading. My mother had never attended school and she didn't understand me. To tell the truth, I didn't understand her anymore. My education was a dear thing but it had cost me greatly. I had lost my place in the world.

≈ *Afterword* ≈

ALTHOUGH GERTRUDE RETURNED to the reservation, she never returned to the joy of her early childhood. While she was at school, she missed her mother and the security of her culture; however, while she was at home she found that she longed for the joys and challenges of academic learning.

Over the next few years, Gertrude struggled to assimilate into reservation life. Finally, at fifteen, she returned to White's Manual Labor Institute and spent the next four years there attending high school. A bright and multitalented student, Gertrude was an excellent violinist, and she excelled in writing and public speaking as well. When she received an offer for financial aid, she decided to continue with her education and attend college.

Upon graduation, she worked as a teacher at the Carlisle Indian School in Pennsylvania, where she wrote several autobiographical short stories. Gertrude wanted to show white people the reality of Indian life. Through education, she hoped to ease some of the prejudice and mistreatment of her people. Her stories were published and received glowing reviews. She continued writing articles and began working on *Old Indian Legends*, a book for children.

After two years, Gertrude left Carlisle Indian School and enrolled at the Boston Conservatory for Music in Massachusetts. She focused on her violin music and continued to write for magazines. But she also questioned whether this was the right path for her. On one hand, she loved her life in the East, yet on the other hand, she felt like she was deserting her people and her culture. Although it was a hard decision,

Gertrude remained home for nineteen months and then left the reservation to attend a boarding school on the Santee Reservation in Nebraska. In this 1890 photograph, Gertrude is the third student from the right in the back row. Photograph courtesy of the Center for Western Studies.

in 1901 Gertrude chose to return to the reservation, where she married another Yankton Sioux and devoted the rest of her life to working for Indian reform.

Gertrude continued to use her gift for words. However, instead of stories, she wrote letters, speeches, books, and articles about Indian reform. She became a well-known Native American leader, working hard to create fair laws for her people.

As an adult, Gertrude often characterized herself as a Sioux warrior. And in a way she was. She fought for her people, working diligently to protect them, to educate them, and to help others understand them. Throughout her life she faced poverty and prejudice, but she never let this stop her. Her voice, both written and spoken, became a powerful tool of positive change for her people.

~ *Bibliography* ~

Andrews, William L., ed. *Classic American Autobiographies*. New York: Penguin Putnam, 1992.

Cooper, Michael L. *Indian School: Teaching the White Man's Way*. New York: Clarion Books, 1999.

Edmunds, R. David., ed. *The New Warriors: Native American Leaders Since 1900*. Lincoln, Nebr.: University of Nebraska Press, 2001.

Hoover, Herbert T. *The Yankton Sioux*. New York: Chelsea House Publishers, 1988.

Littlefield, Holly. *Children of the Indian Boarding Schools*. Minneapolis: Carolrhoda Books, Inc., 2001.

Philip, Neil, ed. *A Braid of Lives: Native American Childhood*. New York: Clarion Books, 2000.

Rappaport, Doreen. *The Flight of Red Bird: The Life of Zitkala-Sä*. New York: Dial Books, 1997.

Shepherd, Donna Walsh. *South Dakota*. New York: Children's Press, 2001.

Terry, Michael 'Bad Hand'. *Daily Life in a Plains Indian Village 1868*. New York: Clarion Books, 1999.

Zitkala-Sä. *American Indian Stories*. Lincoln, Nebr.: University of Nebraska Press, 1985.

Index

❧❧

(Note: Page numbers in italics indicate photographs and paintings.)

DON'T MISS THESE OTHER FULCRUM TITLES BY WESTERN WOMEN WRITERS

FULCRUM PUBLISHING 〰 16100 Table Mountain Parkway, Suite 300 〰 Golden, CO 80403
303-277-1623 〰 FAX 303-279-7111

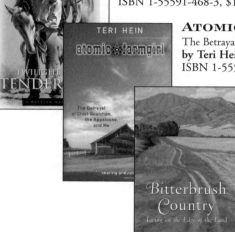

A ROAD OF HER OWN
Women's Journeys in the West
Edited by Marlene Blessing
ISBN 1-55591-307-5, $24.95 HC

TWILIGHT OF THE TENDERFOOT
A Western Memoir
by Diane Ackerman
ISBN 1-55591-468-3, $16.95 PB

ATOMIC FARMGIRL
The Betrayal of Chief Qualchan, the Appaloosa, and Me
by Teri Hein
ISBN 1-55591-443-8, $22.95 HC

BITTERBRUSH COUNTRY
Living on the Edge of the Land
by Diane Josephy Peavey
ISBN 1-55591-293-1, $22.95 HC

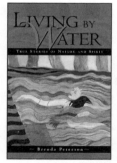

LIVING BY WATER
True Stories of
Nature and Spirit
by Brenda Peterson
ISBN 1-55591-467-5
$16.95 PB

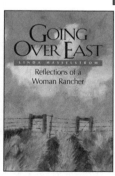

GOING OVER EAST
Reflections of a
Woman Rancher
by Linda Hasselstrom
ISBN 1-55591-141-2
$15.95 PB

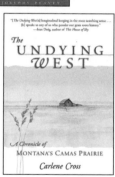

THE UNDYING WEST
A Chronicle of
Montana's Camas Prairie
by Carlene Cross
ISBN 1-55591-432-2
$16.95 PB

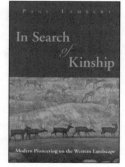

IN SEARCH OF KINSHIP
Modern Pioneering on the
Western Landscape
by Page Lambert
ISBN 1-55591-224-9
$16.95 PB
ISBN 1-55591-266-4
$23.95 HC

To order call 800-992-2908 or visit www.fulcrum-books.com 〰 Also available through your local bookstore.